Veteran journalist and North Shore resident Joel Brown will treat you to a knowing introduction to the special places and rich, sometimes offbeat, traditions of the region.

From the foreword by Annie C. Harris
of Essex Heritage

Joel Brown is a terrific writer who knows the North Shore inside and out – and what makes it special.

Kerry Drohan
Former Globe North editor

For Rosemary, always

More info:
essexbywayguide.com

Also by Joel Brown:
Mermaid Blues (2011)
Mirror Ball Man (2010)

Paper cut images © 2012 Dylan Metrano
Cover design by Greg Freeman
Author photo © 2010 Rosemary Krol

*The information in this book is accurate to the best
of my knowledge, but no guarantee is implied or intended.*

First edition 2012
Printed in the United States of America

ISBN 978-1479313402

ESSEX COASTAL BYWAY GUIDE

HISTORY, CULTURE & NATURE
ON THE NORTH SHORE

JOEL BROWN

TABLE OF CONTENTS

FOREWORD

For nearly four centuries, visitors have been drawn to the coast of Essex County, Massachusetts. Their interactions with the land and sea – the natural elements that define this distinctive region – form a narrative that is at once uniquely local and nationally significant. Fortunately, many of the historical, natural, and cultural touchstones of the past still await the travelers of today.

The Essex Coastal Scenic Byway guides visitors and residents on an eighty-five-mile journey of discovery though one of the country's most picturesque and historically important regions: Boston's legendary North Shore.

Set against a backdrop of rocky shorelines and New England's largest salt marsh, the Byway features mile after mile of breathtaking vistas, working harbors, quaint villages, world-class art and culture, and distinctive local food, shops and lodging. Recreational adventures such as hiking, biking, paddling, and swimming abound at the Byway's numerous parks, trails, waterways and beaches. Sail a historic schooner!

Veteran journalist and North Shore resident Joel Brown will treat you to a knowing introduction to the special places and rich, sometimes offbeat, traditions of the region. Users of this guide will be enthralled by the quantity and quality of the buildings and landscapes that tell the story of the role the region played in the nation's settlement, maritime history and industrialization.

As the book makes clear, the region's historical penchant for innovation offers the traveler a broad range of experiences from which to choose.

Journey with Joel to the port cities of Salem, site of the infamous 1692 witch trials and a center of global commerce during the "Golden Age of Sail"; Gloucester, a busy fishing and arts community founded in 1623 and featured in the movie *The Perfect Storm*; and Newburyport, a historic shipbuilding and trade port renowned for its restored downtown.

The nation's oldest houses can be found in Ipswich, along with Castle Hill, a seaside mansion with fifty-nine rooms and expansive landscaped grounds. Contemporary cultural happenings run the gamut from curated exhibitions at local repositories like the Lynn Museum, to art exhibitions in historic settings such as the Marblehead Arts Association, to new musical offerings such as those staged at the Shalin Liu Performance Center on the Rockport waterfront.

With eco-tourism in mind, Joel gives the region's abundant natural resources their due with insights on marsh ecology, publicly accessible land trust properties, and our love affair with native clams.

As you learn more about our coastal region you'll begin to understand why the U.S. Congress made it part of the Essex National Heritage Area. Designated in 1996, the five-hundred-square-mile Heritage Area is one of forty-nine heritage partnership parks of the National Park Service. And as the Area's nonprofit steward, the Essex National Heritage Commission works with the Byway communities and others to leverage their heritage, business and human resources to generate economic and quality-of-life benefits.

Welcome to Boston's North Shore. As I hope you will discover from Joel Brown's book and your own exploration, we truly offer the best of coastal New England!

Annie C. Harris
Executive Director
Essex National Heritage Commission

ESSEX NATIONAL
HERITAGE AREA

INTRODUCTION

I grew up near Essex County, Massachusetts, and visited the North Shore often. I remember school field trips to see the treasures at what is now the Peabody Essex Museum, a family outing to strange and wonderful Hammond Castle, and a summer camp jaunt to the beach on Plum Island – in greenhead fly season, unfortunately.

When I was in college, we drove to Newburyport, its revival just beginning, to hear folk singers at The Grog. Soon after, a friend invited me to his family's annual clambake on a quiet Cape Ann cove, and I've been going back for thirty years.

I fell for the North Shore's unique mix of history, culture, scenic beauty and seafood long before I moved here.

The Essex Coastal Scenic Byway links thirteen communities that touch the Atlantic Ocean, from Lynn and Salem in the south to Gloucester and Rockport on Cape Ann and on north to Newburyport. Formally designated by the state and promoted by the non-profit Essex National Heritage Commission, the Byway leads travelers to picturesque downtowns and busy working harbors, along sandy beaches and rocky shores.

The North Shore's prominent role in history arose from the challenges and opportunities of living near the high-tide line. Abundant cod attracted many early settlers. Ships sailing from Salem, Gloucester and Newburyport made the area a global maritime power from the seventeenth century into the twentieth. Their crews fished the Grand Banks, traded with East Asia and plundered a few British ships along the way. Some took part in the infamous Triangle Trade. When, or rather, *if* they came home, their captains and owners built grand mansions, business dynasties, schools and more with proceeds from their voyages.

Time marches on, of course. Steamships and railroads eventually took the cargo trade from our clipper ships and schooners, and the wharves fell silent. Fishing remains a significant industry, notably in

Gloucester, but at a fraction of its former size. Building wooden ships is a heritage craft practiced by a handful of devoted custodians.

The "cultural economy" rules today, but it, too, floats on salt water. Historic mansions and treasures from the age of sail anchor the tourist trade. Glorious scenery and ecological richness draw beach-goers, artists and nature lovers. Whale watches sail from seemingly every harbor.

Congress established the Essex National Heritage Area in 1996 to sustain and promote the county's unique sense of place. The Essex National Heritage Commission, better known as Essex Heritage, works with the National Park Service and other public and private groups to make that happen. They give grants, foster partnerships, and draw thousands of visitors with their free Trails & Sails weekends every year. They took the lead in creating the Byway, and without Essex Heritage this book would not exist.

Four other non-profit groups are key to preserving the area's resources, sometimes in collaboration.

The Trustees of Reservations preserve properties of "exceptional scenic, historic, and ecological value" across Massachusetts. The group welcomes the public at more than a hundred sites statewide, fourteen of them on the North Shore, including the grand Crane Estate in Ipswich.

Essex County Greenbelt works to conserve farmland, wildlife habitat and scenic views in the county. The group, headquartered at the Allyn Cox Reservation in Essex, has preserved more than 15,000 acres of pasture, forest and marsh.

Mass Audubon protects the natural environment and wildlife throughout Massachusetts. It is the largest private owner of conserved land in the state, including more than 2,500 acres at a dozen sites on or near the Byway. Audubon's Joppa Flats Education Center in New-buryport is a magnet for birders and eco-tourists of all stripes.

Historic New England calls itself "a museum of cultural history that collects and preserves buildings, landscapes, and objects." The group maintains eight sites on the Byway, ranging from simple early-Colonial homes to the rococo glories of Beauport.

I gradually learned about all these efforts after my wife and I returned to New England in 1998. Seeking salt air after a decade in the Midwest, we landed in Newburyport and stayed.

As a freelance journalist, I've written nearly two hundred features about the North Shore for the *Boston Globe*. I've kayaked the marshes, sailed the coast, biked and hiked and bird-watched, sometimes for a story and sometimes just for fun.

From all this comes an appreciation of what makes the North Shore special and how its seemingly disparate parts fit together. This book is my attempt to translate that understanding into useful intelligence for visitors, whether they come from Paris or Kansas City, the far side of Boston or just the far end of the Byway.

This is not a history book nor a typical travel guide. It's more like the conversation you would have with a friend who lives here, someone who'd tell you what not to miss and why, and maybe share the back story that the official history skips over.

The North Shore is a special place. We've stretched out on the sand on Plum Island at 4 a.m. to watch a meteor shower, joined the cheering at an old-style schooner launch in Essex on a sunny afternoon, and gotten caught in a Halloween-night zombie traffic jam in Salem. I hope this book will help you to enjoy life here as much as we do, whether you come for a day, a week or forever.

Joel Brown
Newburyport, July 2012

USING THIS BOOK

The Essex Coastal Scenic Byway runs from Lynn in the south to Newburyport in the north. At least, that's the direction a majority of visitors are expected to travel, so that's how I've organized this book.

Each chapter covers a single Byway city or town, with the exception of the one on Plum Island. The text highlights non-profit venues such as museums, historic sites and nature preserves. A handful of iconic businesses get their due, as well as such essential topics of North Shore knowledge as fried clams and the greenhead fly.

Many destinations described here are directly on the Byway route, and most others are only a short detour away. I've included street addresses, phone numbers and websites where appropriate, as well as tips on admission prices, parking and getting around. (For starters, don't park in a resident-sticker parking spot at any North Shore beach. Just don't.)

The back of the book offers a few suggested itineraries, a list of Byway visitor centers and other useful information. Hours, prices and other details are subject to change without notice. You can find lots more information at the official website, *www.CoastalByway.org.*

TV newscasters, politicians and people from elsewhere in Massachusetts tend to use "the North Shore" to refer to everything north of Boston and east of Lowell. This book sticks to the more literal standard of Essex County towns that are actually on the coast. Also, here "Cape Ann" refers only to the landmass east of the Annisquam River, containing Rockport and much of Gloucester.

Despite the popular caricature of the taciturn Yankee, the easiest way to learn a new shortcut or find today's best price on lobster rolls is to ask a local. Although not *officially* designated as guides, anyone wearing a faded Red Sox cap is likely to be able to answer your questions. That might even be me.

J.B.

1/LYNN

The Essex Coastal Scenic Byway starts here, and Lynn Shore Drive offers a vista of sand, surf and sea. But Lynn's history resembles that of a Merrimack River mill town more than any of its North Shore neighbors.

The area was first known as Saugus, a Native American name, which changed when minister Samuel Whiting arrived from King's Lynn, England, in 1637. By some accounts, the first shoemakers in town were already at work then, and by the early nineteenth century, shoe shops and tanneries were well on the way to replacing agriculture as the community's economic engine.

Present-day Lynn was incorporated in 1850, and by then two other developments had already begun to shape the city's future. The arrival of the Eastern Railroad in 1838 made Central Square and its train station the focus of a growing urban center. And the invention of the shoe-sewing machine a decade later meant that mass production of footwear soon replaced the cottage industry run by local artisans. By the 1880s, a huge influx of European immigrants was arriving to work in Lynn's famous shoe factories and live in its tenements. Two catastrophic fires in the latter half of the century simply meant that downtown was rebuilt bigger and better.

Lynn shoe magnates were among early investors in local inventor Elihu Thomson's Thomson-Houston Electric Company. That firm merged with Schenectady-based Edison Electric in 1892 to form General Electric, which remains one of the city's largest employers today. GE Aviation's Lynn River Works complex supplies jet engines to both military and civilian customers around the world.

The local shoe industry began to decline in the early twentieth century, and Lynn's population peaked at about 100,000 in 1930. By then, the city already had a freewheeling reputation. Even today, most Boston-area youth learn the old rhyme that begins, "Lynn, Lynn, city of sin..." By the 1980s the city center was enduring tough economic times, beset by drugs, crime and vacant buildings.

A concerted effort at revitalization has made headway since then, luring young professionals to live in restored industrial buildings. The train station in Central Square, a commuter rail stop, remains a key selling point. The state has recently recognized the Central Exchange Cultural District in Lynn, where the Lynn Museum, LynnArts, RAW Art Works and other groups create cultural experiences shared across the city's diverse populations and age groups. The influx of new immigrants, primarily Hispanic and Asian, has added vitality. But Lynn has yet to reach its full potential.

Byway route: *The Byway begins at the busy intersection of Broad Street and the Lynnway and offers two routes through town.*

Downtown route: Head north, following Route 1A/Route 129 along Broad Street, Lewis Street and Ocean Street. Follow Ocean when it turns right after a short distance. When it forks, bear left and continue onto Route 129 into Swampscott.

Shore route: Turn east on the Lynnway, navigate one of our infamous Massachusetts traffic rotaries, and head north on scenic Lynn Shore Drive until it merges with Route 129, just over the Swampscott border.

High Rock Reservation

If you want an overview of Lynn and Boston Harbor, this promontory in the Highlands neighborhood rises nearly 200 feet above sea level. The centerpiece of the three-acre park is the 85-foot High

Rock Tower, designed by H.K. Wheeler of Lynn and dedicated in 1906. Atop the refurbished tower is an observatory that's home to the city's 12-inch Meade telescope, where visitors can explore the moon's surface, the rings of Saturn, and the galaxies of the night sky. Volunteers organize monthly public viewing nights.

The park is intimately associated with one of Lynn's most famous and unusual families. Natives of Milford, N.H., John, Jesse, Asa and Judson Hutchinson were performing here as singers by 1840. With Jesse replaced by their sister, Abby, they toured as the Hutchinson Family Singers and sang in support of what were then considered "radical" causes, such as temperance, abolitionism and women's suffrage. Family members also founded Hutchinson, Kansas. You can learn more about them at the Lynn Museum.

After purchasing High Rock in the 1840s, the family built the first tower on the site, as well as a stone cottage that still stands. They held rallies and concerts at High Rock during the Civil War; the tower burned down, apparently accidentally, during a victory celebration at the end of that conflict. In a final act of public-minded-ness, in 1904 John W. Hutchinson gave the park to the city, which agreed to build a new tower on the site.

Circuit Avenue, off High Rock Street, Lynn

www.ci.lynn.ma.us

Lynn Museum & Historical Society

A visit to the Lynn Museum in summer 2012 provided the perfect example of an institution representing a changing community.

In an upper gallery, the exhibit "Shoes: A Step Back In Time" focused on Lynn's history as a footwear capital. Wall displays highlighted the industry's enormous impact in the city at the beginning of the twentieth century and the European immigrants who flocked to work here. The exhibit featured a lasting machine and even some fancy shoes to try on. But you only had to turn a corner to find the solemn "More Than A Number: Stories From Lynn," featuring the often horrifying narratives of dozens of Cambodians who fled the Killing Fields of the Khmer Rouge and became part of the city's new wave of immigrants.

Founded in 1897 and housed in a restored building in Central Square, the Lynn Museum embraces both serious history and local kitsch, and hosts a variety of community-centered events and exhibits.

One of the gems of its collection is a gorgeous circa-1910 oil portrait by the great American impressionist Frank W. Benson, *Mrs. Virginia N. Johnson and her Sons, Benjamin, Jr., and Richard*. Mrs. Johnson and her husband Benjamin Sr. were founding members of the society, and Benjamin, Jr. donated the painting when he grew up. It's a piece that could easily hang in the Museum of Fine Arts, but it's here, not far from a Harry Agganis baseball card, a Boyd's potato chip can and a J85 jet engine built at General Electric's nearby plant.

Besides the Benson painting, the other must-see piece here is the *Shoe Medallion*, created to represent the city at the 1893 Columbian Exposition in Chicago. Its large frame is filled with a wheel of 234 miniature leather soles with distinctive decorative designs, each representing a different Lynn shoe manufacturer.

The most popular item in the gift shop, however, seems to be the "I'm a fluffernutter...I'm from Lynn" t-shirts, sold here exclusively to celebrate the locally made product Marshmallow Fluff. General admission is $5.

590 Washington Street, Lynn
781-581-6200
www.lynnmuseum.org

Lynn Shore & Nahant Beach Reservation

The state acquired numerous private properties in the early 1900s to create the two abutting beach preserves, presumably to offer weekend recreation to the thousands toiling in nearby factories.

Nahant Beach, known locally as Long Beach, stretches along the entire ocean side of the narrow, more than mile-long causeway that connects the town of Nahant to the mainland. There are two bathhouses and extensive parking along the beach. This is a great place for swimming and sunbathing, as well as jogging, walking and bike-riding along the flat, straight causeway. Because of its breezy location, with open water on either side, serious kite-flyers also favor Long Beach. A boat ramp and ballfields are on the harbor side of the causeway. To get to Long Beach, follow the Lynnway to the rotary at the end and bear right, following the signs for Nahant.

You can also go the rest of the way around the rotary and come out on Lynn Shore Drive. Along this seaside promenade, you'll find broad, sandy King's Beach as well as scenic overlooks at Woodbury Point and Red Rock Park. The latter is the site of summer concerts and other activities. There are no facilities at King's Beach, but there is parking along Lynn Shore Drive.

781-485-2803
www.mass.gov/dcr

Lynn Woods Reservation

The second-largest municipal park in the United States takes up nearly one-fifth of the city's land area. This 2,200-acre oasis was founded in 1881 and includes thirty miles of wooded trails for hiking, running and mountain-biking. There are three reservoirs, an amphitheater for events, a 48-foot stone observation tower, a rose garden and more. There is also an active Friends of Lynn Woods group.

The park is also known for the storied Dungeon Rock, where some believe a pirate's treasure is still buried. This dates to the 1658 appearance of a sinister black ship in Lynn Harbor, from which four men rowed ashore with a chest, headed up the Saugus River and made camp near the Saugus Iron Works. Three of these brigands were captured by the British and hung. The fourth, Thomas Veal, escaped and set up camp in a cave, becoming an accepted part of the community until an earthquake toppled a huge rock, sealing his home shut with him inside. Hence: Dungeon Rock. Why he would live in a cave if he possessed a pirate's treasure is, of course, another question. But in the 1800s a family of spiritualists spent nearly three decades unsuccessfully trying to excavate the booty, even selling tickets to tour their diggings to finance the work. Their tunnels remain today.

As with any such large park, there are a variety of regulations on its use, and it's best to consult the websites before setting out. The main entrance is on the west side of the reservation, on Pennybrook Road, and there is also an east entrance, on Great Woods Road.

781-477-7123

www.ci.lynn.ma.us

www.flw.org

Mary Baker Eddy Home

Christian Science founder Mary Baker Eddy moved to this house in 1875, two years after divorcing her second husband, Daniel Patterson. More importantly, it had been nine years since an experience in their Swampscott apartment led her to believe a better understanding of God could heal more effectively than man's medicine.

She worked on her writing in a small attic room here, and by the end of the year, she had published the 1,000-copy first edition of her book "Science and Health." The essential "textbook" of Christian Science, this volume was later called "Science and Health with Key to the Scriptures."

At the time, she was using the name Mary Baker Glover, after her first husband, the late George Washington Glover. She hung a sign above the home's second-floor windows proclaiming it as "Mary B. Glover's Christian Scientists' Home," and began meeting with groups of students.

On New Year's Day, 1877, she married Asa Gilbert Eddy, her third husband, in the parlor of the house. Two years later, she formally founded the Church of Christ, Scientist, and in 1882, they moved to Boston to advance her teaching.

The house is now owned by the Longyear Museum of Brookline, "an independent historical museum dedicated to advancing the understanding of the life and work of Mary Baker Eddy." Exterior renovation and accessibility projects were completed in 2011. Planning for restoration and interpretation of the inside are under way.

For now, the house is open for visitors only one morning a month, from May through October, and reservations are required at least 48 hours in advance.

12 Broad Street, Lynn
800-277-8943 x100
www.longyear.org

2/SWAMPSCOTT

Swampscott was settled in 1629 and became the site of the first tannery in the Massachusetts Bay Colony. A modest fishing community, Swampscott also had a share in Lynn's footwear industry. It split off from Lynn to incorporate on its own in 1852. The decades that followed saw it shape a more prosperous identity that persists today.

Like many North Shore communities, Swampscott enjoyed success as a summer resort beginning later in the nineteenth century, with grand hotels hosting wealthy and famous guests, some of whom built elaborate summer "cottages" along what was known as the Gold Coast. Most famously, president Calvin Coolidge and First Lady Grace Coolidge arrived by train in 1925 to establish the Summer White House at White Court on Little's Point Road. The estate is now the home of Marian Court College, a two-year private institution.

Swampscott's destination status disappeared after the Crash of 1929. Most of the hotels and largest mansions are long gone, lost to fire and storms or simply torn down to make way for other kinds of development. The town is now a quiet residential enclave, beloved by residents for its ocean views and small-town atmosphere.

Swampscott's other claim to fame is as the home of the lobster pot – that's a lobster trap to those of you from elsewhere. Ebenezer Thorndike invented the trap with its one-way entrance in 1808, and the same basic design is still in use today, though with many refinements and modern materials. A closely related advance was the design of the Swampscott Dory, a sturdy craft for lobstermen alone on the water pulling up lobster pots from the bottom.

The Fish House, at Humphrey Street on Fisherman's Beach, is said to be the only working municipal fish house on the East Coast. Built in 1896 on land taken by eminent domain, its construction was an attempt to replace ramshackle structures along the water that marred the view for tourists and wealthy summer residents. Now on the national register of Historic Places, it is home to the Swampscott Yacht Club on the second floor.

Byway route: *Follow Route 129 north along the coastline to Marblehead.*

Beach Bluff Park

A small oceanfront park at Preston Beach on the Marblehead town line, highlighted by the Sun Circle, an installation of large rocks like a small-scale Stonehenge. Four times a year, at the solstice and the equinox, sunrise ceremonies are held to mark the change of seasons.

The family of John and Ruth Blodgett donated the land for public use in 1993, and the park is maintained by the neighborhood Clifton Improvement Association. A gathering place and fishing spot with paths for strolling, it is used more by residents than visitors, but offers a nice spot to picnic or just take in the view. Parking is available in a lot across the street.

499 Atlantic Avenue, Swampscott
www.ciabeachbluff.org

Elihu Thomson House/Town Hall

This sturdy brick Georgian revival mansion was the home of inventor Elihu Thomson from 1889 to his death in 1937, and now serves as the Swampscott Town Hall.

Thomson was born in Manchester, England in 1853, the son of a mill mechanic, and emigrated to America with his family in 1858.

While teaching high school in Philadelphia in the 1870s, he and a fellow teacher named Edwin J. Houston built a practical electric arc lighting system. In 1882 a group of Lynn, Massachusetts, businessmen purchased their company and changed the name to the Thomson-Houston Electric Company. In 1892 Thomson's Company merged with the Edison General Electric Company to form General Electric.

The company moved to Schenectady, N.Y., but Thomson remained behind, exploring his interests in various scientific disciplines at his labs in Lynn and at his home here. The house was originally built with an observatory, which no longer exists. Thomson held nearly 700 patents and remained active until his death at age 83. He is credited with advocating for pure research at companies like General Electric.

In 1944, his family presented the property to the town as a gift in his memory. It now serves all the typical functions of a New England town hall, including as a meeting place for the selectmen. Thomson artifacts here include a photograph of him and his wife and a small desk that was once his.

22 Monument Avenue, Swampscott
781-596-8850
www.town.swampscott.ma.us

John Humphrey Memorial House

John Humphrey was the first deputy governor of the Massachusetts Bay Colony, under Gov. John Winthrop. The house was built in 1637 on Elwood Road (a plaque marks the site) and moved to its present location in 1891. The house is preserved and maintained by the Swampscott Historical Society, which hosts lectures and displays historical artifacts there. The eclectic collection includes the propeller of a plane that was built in town before World War I, as well as paintings, etchings and photographs of earlier eras.

There are guided tours for school groups, and the house is open to the public on every July 4.

99 Paradise Road, Swampscott
781-599-1297

Mary Baker Eddy Home

This is where the then-Mary B. Patterson experienced the sudden recovery that started her on the road to founding Christian Science.

In late 1865, always sickly Mary and her second husband, Daniel Patterson, rented an upstairs apartment in this house. In February 1866, on her way to a Temperance meeting, Mary fell on an icy sidewalk and was brought home with apparent serious injuries, barely able to move. Lying on a cot in her kitchen, she spent her time praying and reading the Bible. An account of Jesus healing the sick inspired her to get to her feet and cross the room to a chair. She attributed this recovery entirely to the power of prayer, and from there began to develop her belief in healing through a higher understanding of God.

Shortly after the incident, the house was sold. The Pattersons moved, and she and Daniel divorced in 1873. Two years later, while living in Lynn, she published "Science and Health."

Today the house is maintained by the Longyear Museum of Brookline. The house and remaining grounds have been restored, and the upstairs apartment is furnished in typical nineteenth-century style. The house is open May through October, from Wednesday through Sunday.

23 Paradise Rd., Swampscott
800-277-8943 x100
www.longyear.org

Olmsted Historic District

After opening his office in Brookline in 1883, the visionary landscape architect Frederick Law Olmsted designed Boston's Emerald Necklace as well as the grounds of McLean Hospital, where he spent the last years of his life. But he also left his mark on Swampscott.

Olmsted was invited to town in 1888 by the Swampscott Land Trust to design one of the North Shore's first subdivisions. Perhaps fittingly, Olmsted went to work turning the 130-acre seaside Mudge Estate into 191 house lots according to his egalitarian vision. The streets wind gently through rolling hills and shrubbery, balancing public and private, civilization and nature.

A few modern homes aside, the district remains much as it was when it was completed early in the twentieth century, although the gravel streets have been paved to accommodate cars. You can print out a map and brochure from *essexheritage.org*. The entire district is now on the National Register of Historic Places. Enter via Monument Avenue.

Off Burrill Street, Swampscott

3/MARBLEHEAD

Marblehead was settled in 1629, although by most accounts a few colonists arrived in the area earlier, trying to escape Salem's strict Puritan rule. The settlers got along well with the local Naumkeg tribe, but disease, probably smallpox, decimated the native population. By mid-century, Marblehead had been granted independence from Salem and was becoming a busy fishing port. Maritime prowess has been central to the town's history ever since, although today its renown has more to do with yacht races than cod or cannonballs.

Marblehead captains and crews distinguished themselves in the Revolutionary War and the War of 1812. The schooner Hannah was the first ship commissioned into the Continental Army by George Washington in 1775, and so the town considers itself the birthplace of the U.S. Navy. Hannah was owned by local merchant John Glover and named for his wife. Gen. Glover also commanded a regiment of Marblehead men, many with nautical experience, that served nobly in the Revolutionary cause and ferried Washington across the Delaware to attack Trenton in 1776.

A devastating Grand Banks storm in 1846 wiped out much of the fishing fleet that employed the men in peacetime, perhaps hastening a shift away from that industry. For several decades Marblehead had a significant shoe-making industry, but catastrophic fires in 1877 and 1888 destroyed most of the factories.

Like much of the North Shore, Marblehead's coastline attracted an affluent summer crowd in the latter half of the nineteenth century. The harbor became a major yachting center, known today for its
venerable yacht clubs and annual midsummer Race Week. Today the
narrow, curving streets of the historic downtown are dotted with shops
and galleries that serve well-off locals and visitors alike.

Byway route: *Take Route 129/Atlantic Avenue to Ocean Avenue. Go straight across Ocean and continue on Atlantic to Washington
Street.*

*Turn right on Washington and pass through the downtown,
then a few quick turns: left on Mugford, left on Elm, left on Spring and
right on Pleasant. Stay on Pleasant as it becomes Route 114, and follow 114 north into Salem.*

Abbot Hall

Both the Town Hall and an historical museum, this impressive
brick structure features a clock tower that juts above the local horizon.

Here you'll find the original version of Archibald MacNeal
Willard's painting *The Spirit of '76*, which depicts two drummers and a
wounded fife player marching forward across a Revolutionary War
battlefield, with an early stars-and-stripes behind them. Also known as
"Yankee Doodle," the painting was produced in several subsequent
versions by Willard and has been copied, parodied and repurposed
countless times. But its display in a room regularly used for selectmen's meetings surely says something about the simple power of the
American ideal.

A variety of other items of local significance are on display.
Here you'll find a plaque, discovered at the Philadelphia Navy Yard,
supporting Marblehead's claim to be the "Birthplace of the American
Navy." Call ahead for hours, which vary by season.

188 Washington St., Marblehead
781-631-0000
www.marblehead.org

Chandler Hovey Park

Follow Ocean Avenue to Follett Street at the eastern tip of Marblehead Neck, and at the end you'll find this nearly four-acre park, named for the local resident who bought the land from the federal government and donated it to the town in 1948. Grassy lawns, rocky shores, tidepools, free parking, picnic tables, even restrooms – all that, and the park's best feature is still the panoramic view, encompassing Marblehead Harbor and a wide swath of North Shore waters reaching to Manchester and Beverly. A great spot for a picnic.

The park is also known as Lighthouse Point for its most notable feature, Marblehead Light. Opinions are divided over the appearance of the 105-foot tower, which is a cast-iron skeleton bearing little resemblance to a classic New England lighthouse. It was built in 1895 to replace a smaller beacon dating to 1835. A central iron column contains a narrow spiral staircase to the top. The Coast Guard still maintains the light as an aid to navigation, and the tower is not open to the public.

Follett and Kimball Streets, Marblehead
www.marblehead.org

Crocker Park

The best view of Marblehead Harbor, except for the one from the deck of your own yacht. Grab a bench or a square of lawn for a front row seat on all the maritime comings and goings.

The site was originally known as Bartoll's Head, but the three-acre park was eventually named after Uriel Crocker, who donated the land to the town in 1885. There's a gazebo, restrooms, and a stairway down to the water's edge.

Regular concerts enliven the scene in the summer, and the park is a popular site for weddings, photo shoots and other special occasions. As it is located off a quiet residential street, parking may be scarce.

Front Street, Marblehead
www.marblehead.org

Devereaux Beach

The town's most popular beach is at the beginning of the causeway to Marblehead Neck, by the site of the seventeenth-century home of John Devereaux. Inspired by an evening at the farmhouse, Henry Wadsworth Longfellow wrote his 1850 poem "The Fire of Driftwood," which seems to be a contemplation of mortality. Longfellow visited in 1846, and the driftwood might have been an evocation of the ships wrecked in the terrible storm of that year – an influence on the poem's bittersweet mood? In any case, the house is long gone.

The five-and-a-half acre beach complex also includes a picnic pavilion, snack bar, restrooms and a parking lot where a resident sticker will save you a few bucks. And there are excellent views across the sparkling waters of Massachusetts Bay.

Ocean Avenue, Marblehead
www.marblehead.org

Fort Sewall

Fort Sewall had its greatest moment in April 1814, when the U.S.S. Constitution limped into Marblehead Harbor with a split mast, pursued by two British frigates. The citizens of the town rushed to man the cannons at Fort Sewall, and the British turned away. In 1997, Old Ironsides returned to Marblehead to commemorate the moment.

Founded in 1644 on a piece of land known as Gale's Head, and enlarged repeatedly up through the Civil War, the fort is named in honor of Judge Samuel Sewall, a prominent citizen and Justice of the Massachusetts Supreme Court. Much of the fort's earthwork structure still exists, including the underground stockade. The city accepted it as a town park circa 1890, when the harbor no longer needed protecting.

Now a popular spot for everything from dog walking to annual military reenactments, the park offers a lovely view of the harbor and the waters beyond. There are benches, restrooms and a small parking area, plus a beach used by local fishermen to land their skiffs.

East end of Front Street, Marblehead
www.marblehead.org

Jeremiah Lee Mansion

The Marblehead Museum and Historical Society maintains the Jeremiah Lee Mansion, an imposing colonial Georgian home at 161 Washington St. Manchester native Lee was a leading businessman in Pre-Revolutionary Marblehead and one of the wealthiest men in Massachusetts. He owned twenty-one ships, including fishing schooners and cargo vessels that sailed European routes. But he was also an undercover hero of the Revolution, procuring arms for the rebels and meeting secretly with John Hancock and Sam Adams.

Lee and his family lived on Union Street until 1768, when he built this three-story wooden structure with a façade designed to look like stone. It was one of the most opulent homes in the Colonies. Lee died in 1775, however, and by 1804 his fortune was gone, and the home passed to the Marblehead Bank.

The historical society bought it for $5,000 in 1909 and has operated it as a museum ever since.

The interior is remarkably unchanged from when Lee lived there, with original hand-painted English wallpaper murals, ceramic fireplace tiles, elaborate mahogany woodwork and furniture by Colonial craftsmen.

The entry hall features period reproductions of John Singleton Copley's 1769 portraits of Lee and his wife Martha (the originals are in Wadsworth Atheneum Museum of Art in Hartford, Conn.). Martha was the sister-in-law of Robert "King" Hooper, whose nearby house is listed on the next page.

House tours are available seasonally, usually Tuesday through Saturday from June through October. The Marblehead Garden Club has maintained elaborate, historically-inspired gardens on the property since 1936. The Marblehead Museum galleries are right across the street.

161 Washington St., Marblehead
781-631-1768
www.marbleheadmuseum.org

King Hooper Mansion

The original portion of the King Hooper Mansion was built by candle maker Greenfield Hooper in 1728. His son Robert, a wealthy shipping merchant, added the three-story front section of the house in 1745. Robert was such a success in the shipping and fish trades that he earned the affectionate nickname "King." No surprise that the street outside is Hooper Street.

The mansion is now the home of the Marblehead Art Association, founded in 1922, which now has more than 600 members. Several rooms of the mansion are used as galleries with rotating exhibits by local artists and artisans, as well as a gift shop. The old floors, walls and fireplaces make an interesting contrast with the contemporary painting styles and digital photographs. There's a lovely rear garden.

8 Hooper St., Marblehead
781-631-2608
www.marbleheadarts.org

Marblehead Museum galleries

Compared to its magnificent Jeremiah Lee Mansion across the street, the headquarters of the Marblehead Museum and Historical Society is a modest venue. Visit one of the rotating exhibits on local history in the front room, and you may find yourself striking up a conversation with a volunteer performing clerical tasks at a desk around the corner.

But there's a hidden treasure here.

Climb the stairs to the second floor, and you'll find yourself in the J.O.J. Frost Folk Art Gallery, a collection of truly strange and wonderful works painted by an idiosyncratic local character with an unforgettable story. It's a must-see.

John Orne Johnson Frost loved Marblehead. He was born there in 1852 and grew up near the harbor. He went to sea on a Grand Banks schooner at age 16, but left that brutal work after just two voyages, following a terrifying snowstorm. Back on dry land, he married Annie Lillibridge and went to work in her father's restaurant at Washington and Darling Streets. He also helped his wife sell cut flowers from a wheelbarrow and at their home.

Sometime after his beloved Annie's death in 1919, Frost began painting scenes of Marblehead history and life at sea, using scrap wood and house paint. He also created many wood carvings, especially of local fish species. He had no artistic training, and his pictures have flat perspectives and misspelled inscriptions that mark them clearly as outsider art. But they can also be startlingly vivid, most notably the large image depicting one terrible day in local maritime history: "1846 Gale 11 vessels lost 65 men 43 widows 155 fatherless children ... And the sea gave up the dead wich (sic) were in it."

Frost tried to sell his art from the wheelbarrow for less than a dollar a painting, but met with little success. His attempt to start a "museum" in his 11 Pond St. backyard did no better. Upon his death in 1928, the family gave much of his work to the historical society. An exhibit at the Lee Mansion in the 1940s began to create appreciation of the works. Now collectors, galleries and other institutions have also acquired and exhibited Frost paintings, which sell for much more than he could have imagined.

In a sense, Frost was Marblehead's own Vincent van Gogh, his works valued only posthumously. Even though they were painted in the twentieth century, his pictures will make you feel as close to local history as any masterpiece in nearby museums.

The galleries are open year-round, although on a reduced schedule November through May.

170 Washington St., Marblehead
781-631-1768
www.marbleheadmuseum.org

Marblehead Neck Wildlife Sanctuary

Mass Audubon owns this little-known oasis, tucked away in the middle of Marblehead Neck at the end of a quiet, dead-end residential street. The 18 acres of woods, trails and wetlands play host to many species of native and migratory birds. During the spring migration, in particular, birds that have flown over the ocean for many miles may find their first rest here. As a result, area birders know the sanctuary as a place to find rarities.

Easy hikes on dirt paths predominate. Audubon Pond is home to many dragonflies and bullfrogs, or at least it was on the day we visited. No bicycles or pets allowed. There is a small parking area. The site is managed by the Ipswich River Wildlife Sanctuary.

Risley Road
978-887-9264
www.massaudubon.org

4/SALEM

In Salem, it's always the season of the witch.

The 1692 witchcraft hysteria among the Puritans still echoes in complicated and often contradictory ways here. The witch hunt was a dark chapter in New England history that cost twenty innocent people their lives, and yet Salem styles itself as Witch City to attract tourism. Even though the point of the story is that *there weren't any witches*.

See? Complicated.

Salem has a lot more to offer than the macabre. There's plenty to see and do arising from the city's history as one of the young nation's great global trade ports. The Peabody Essex Museum is the North Shore's premier cultural institution, and the Salem Maritime National Historic Site offers another major draw.

But the largest crowds come because of what happened after two little girls began to act strangely in Salem Village – now Danvers – in the winter of 1692.

Elizabeth "Betty" Parris, age 9, and her cousin Abigail Williams, 11, screamed and threw fits that neither Betty's minister father nor the local doctor could explain. Scholars still debate possible causes of the girls' odd behavior, from the LSD-like effects of ergot fungus in rye bread to a simple craving for attention. Likely the truth will never be known for certain. But the townspeople of that time quickly settled on a more sinister explanation.

Three outcast women, one of them a slave, were accused of using witchcraft on the girls and jailed. Meanwhile other girls began to
exhibit similar symptoms. The hysteria spread rapidly, and by spring
dozens of alleged witches were locked up on the flimsiest of evidence.
Some suspects confessed under duress or accused others to aid their
own cause. Eventually fourteen women and five men were hanged for
witchcraft, and one man was pressed to death. Others were imprisoned
and died behind bars or saw their lives ruined. Contrary to popular
myth, however, no one was burned at the stake.

The community gradually came to its senses when it was too
late. The prosecutions met with growing denouncement and regret.
Survivors of those executed were compensated. It took until 2001, but
all of the witch-trial victims were eventually declared innocent by the
Commonwealth of Massachusetts.

It was not the only witch hunt in the area in that era, just the
largest. Over the years, the story has been re-examined through lenses
of history, politics, psychology, sexuality, religion and literature. Perhaps the best-known fictional telling is Arthur Miller's 1952 play "The
Crucible," which used the events as an allegory for the McCarthy-era
Red Scare in America. A film version of "The Crucible" was shot in
Ipswich in 1995.

Key witch-trial-related sites in Salem are described in the following pages. Many of the events did not happen within the city's present-day boundaries, however, but in locations that are now part of
Danvers, Peabody and other communities. Information on touring them
is available at the National Park Service visitor center.

First settled in 1626, Salem began as a fishing settlement, with
cod as food and fertilizer. Larger vessels gradually replaced fishing
shallops at the docks, as Salem captains turned their attention to trade,
first with the West Indies and later around the globe.

Salem became as powerful a port as the New World had to offer through the 1700s and particularly after the Revolution. Captains
opened new trade routes with the Indian Ocean and China. Ship owners
and their investors built fortunes on cargoes of cotton and spice and
coffee. They decorated their grand homes with Chinese porcelain and

Asian art and dressed their wives in exotic silks. They also donated many of their finds to the institutions that would become the Peabody Essex Museum.

Like other area ports, Salem took a hit from the embargo act of 1807 and the disruptions of the War of 1812. Although the maritime trade recovered to a degree, the shallow harbor kept away the larger ships of later decades, and Salem's dominance of global trade routes faded. The local economy gradually turned to manufacturing of textiles and shoes, industries that largely evaporated in the twentieth century.

The city of about 40,000 residents is the seat of Essex County government, home to a large business community and fast-growing Salem State University. But tourism is its lifeblood. There's something for every sort of traveler here, from the historic Hawthorne Hotel to a lively local arts scene featuring the Salem Theatre Company, art galleries and the hip Gulu-Gulu Café.

Byway route: *From the Marblehead line, follow 114 north into Salem where it meets 1A. Stay with 1A as it snakes through downtown Salem and on to the Veterans Memorial Bridge, where you cross into Beverly.*

"Bewitched" statue

Pop culture can find a lighter side to anything, even a witch hunt. The ABC sitcom "Bewitched," starring Elizabeth Montgomery as the suburban good witch Samantha, shot parts of six episodes in Salem and Gloucester in summer 1970. When the shows aired that fall, they inspired a boomlet in witch-related tourism here, a spark for an industry that thrives today.

The storyline that links the episodes finds Samantha and her mortal husband Darrin checking into the "Hawthorne Motor Hotel" in Salem so she can defend their "mixed" marriage at a witches' convocation. Seen today on DVD, the shows offer a cheesy and confusing mix of actual locations and California studio sets. In one, Samantha is harassed by a haunted bed-warmer at The House of Seven Gables. Another finds Darrin zapped into the Gloucester Fishermen's Memorial. The storyline concludes with the inevitable detour to 1692, as Samantha faces a witch trial of her own. Credit where due: The episode emphasizes that none of the real-life Salem victims were witches.

In 2005, the cable channel TV Land paid for the "Bewitched" statue, a bronze installed in Lappin Park to mark the show's Salem connection. It depicts Montgomery as Samantha riding a broom in front of the moon, as seen in the show's animated opening. At the time of its installation, the statue aroused opposition from those who felt it trivialized the events of 1692. Opponents were outnumbered by fans at the dedication ceremony, however, and only a single protester was arrested. The controversy seems to have evaporated since.

Essex and Washington Streets, Salem

Gedney House

Wealthy shipwright Eleazer Gedney built the earliest portion of this structure in 1665. He was preparing for his marriage to Elizabeth Turner, whose brother John would build the House of the Seven Gables three years later. Subsequent owners added on to the house, changing the roof line and converting it to a multi-family dwelling.

The structure was being gutted in 1967 when a passerby noticed eighteenth-century paneling in the trash piled up outside. The woman had taken a class with the noted preservationist Abbott Lowell Cummings and quickly recognized the building's true age. She contacted Cummings, who was also assistant director of Historic New England. The property was soon acquired by the group and preserved in raw form for display and study of its architecture, materials and finishes. Which is to say, there are no furnishings or exhibits, only the house itself.

The Gedney House is open for tours during limited hours on the first Saturday of each month, June through October. Visit here, then move on to the nearby Phillips House.

21 High Street, Salem
978-744-0440
www.historicnewengland.org

House of the Seven Gables

The mansion just off busy Derby Street might well have earned historic landmark status without Salem native Nathaniel Hawthorne's novel. But it probably wouldn't have become world famous.

It was built by sea captain and merchant John Turner in 1668 and occupied by his family until it was sold to Captain Samuel Ingersoll in 1782. Ingersoll died at sea and left the property to his daughter Susanna, who often hosted her cousin Hawthorne there. At the time, the renovated house had only three gables, but Hawthorne apparently knew of its earlier state.

The author's great-great grandfather was John Hathorne, a judge in the witch trials, remembered for his accusatory questioning and said to be the only trial official who never recanted his actions. Some say the author added the W to his surname to disassociate himself from his infamous ancestor.

Using the house as setting and the judge as one inspiration, Hawthorne penned the 1851 novel that made it famous. The tale of the fictional Pyncheon family features a gloomy mansion, a hypocritical jurist and a witch's curse, among other Gothic elements. It was an immediate hit.

Philanthropist Caroline Emmerton was inspired by Jane Addams's Hull House in Chicago when she purchased what was then known as the Turner-Ingersoll Mansion in 1908. Banking on the book's fame, she turned the house into a museum, using the proceeds to fund settlement programs for immigrant families arriving in Salem. Also a preservationist, Emmerton worked with architect Joseph Everett Chandler to restore the house, complete with its original seven gables. Some of the renovations were more aimed at pleasing Hawthorne's readers, however, including construction of a hidden staircase and a ground-floor "cent shop" like the one operated by one of the book's characters.

Guided tours explore the real history of the house as well as the novel. A variety of programs are also held inside, such as "Spirits of the Gables," focused on Hawthorne's book, and "Legacy of the Hanging Judge."

Behind the house, a lovely lawn and period-style gardens look out on Salem Harbor.

The house is also the center of its own National Historic District, which includes Hawthorne's Birthplace (circa 1750), The Retire Becket House (1655), The Hooper Hathaway House (1682), The Phippen House (circa 1782), and the Counting House (circa 1830). Most were moved here during the twentieth century from their original locations nearby and are also open for tours.

The House of the Seven Gables is open year-round. As with many Salem attractions, expect crowds during October.

115 Derby Street, Salem
978-744-0991
www.7gables.org

National Park Service
Regional Visitor Center

Here Park Rangers and volunteers will provide you with maps, brochures and anything else you need to plan your time in Salem and elsewhere on the North Shore.

There are modest rotating exhibits, and a theater shows films on subjects such as maritime history and the witch trials. The large gift shop is notable for its selection of books on local topics, some difficult to find elsewhere.

The visitor center is housed in a remodeled 1895 brick "drill shed," all that remains of the old armory of the Second Corps of Cadets of the Massachusetts National Guard. It is across the street from the Peabody Essex Museum and a large parking garage. It's a great place to start your visit, and a regular stop for the Salem Trolley.

Open daily, except for Thanksgiving, Christmas and New Year's Day.

2 New Liberty Street, Salem
(978) 740-1650
www.nps.gov

Peabody Essex Museum

This Salem institution has undergone a vast transformation in the last decade or so. Thanks to Salem seafarers of the eighteenth and early nineteenth centuries, the museum has always had rich collections from China, India and around the Pacific, as well as in Early American decorative and maritime art. But with a new attitude and new building for the new millennium, it has become one of the most vibrant museums in the Boston area, offering creative and ambitious exhibits.

The roots of the Peabody Essex Museum date to the 1799 founding of the East India Marine Society by Salem captains and supercargoes who had sailed beyond the Cape of Good Hope or Cape Horn. (A supercargo is employed by the owner of a ship's cargo to travel onboard and conduct related business.) The society's charter called for creation of a "cabinet of natural and artificial curiosities," from items they had collected in their travels. By 1825, the society had its own building, East India Marine Hall, which remains at the heart of the museum today and contains some of the very first objects collected, along with portraits of society members and an array of figureheads from early sailing ships.

The museum's family tree gets slightly complicated after that.

The East India Marine Society was succeeded by the Peabody Academy of Science, named for benefactor George Peabody. Eventually renamed the Peabody Museum of Salem, it focused on international art and culture.

Meanwhile, two other groups, the Essex Historical Society and the Essex County Natural History Society, were amassing their own collections, focused on local history, culture and nature. In 1848, these two merged to form the Essex Institute.

The interests of the Peabody Museum and the Essex Institute often overlapped. Talk of a union came and went until in 1992, after much study, they merged into the Peabody Essex Museum.

Today the Peabody Essex Museum collections encompass 1.8 million artworks, historic artifacts and other items. The institution's transformation is most powerfully expressed in its building, designed by renowned architect Moshe Safdie and opened in 2003. The soaring modern structure literally embraces East India Marine Hall, offering a vastly expanded array of galleries.

To some, the heart of the museum is its maritime art, which includes numerous paintings of ships at sea and on shore, sailors' tools and artifacts, and portraits of famous names from the era of sail. Unexpected treasures include a recreation of the main salon on Cleopatra's Barge, America's first private ocean-going yacht, built in Salem in 1816, with many of its original furnishings. The equally impressive galleries of American decorative art include such treasures as Charles Osgood's 1840 "Portrait of Nathaniel Hawthorne."

The collection of art and artifacts from China, India, Japan, Korea and other foreign ports is mind-boggling, and it's easy for an aficionado to spend hours admiring the work of a single country or focusing on a specialty like export porcelain or furniture. There's an alabaster model of the Taj Mahal that you can get lost looking at.

Be sure to get a timed ticket for a tour of Yin Yu Tang, the only complete Qing Dynasty house outside China, a strangely transporting experience. This was the home of a prosperous merchant named Huang in China's southeastern Huizhou region, and sheltered family members around its roofless central courtyard for roughly two hundred years until 1982, when the last descendants moved away. In 1997, with the family's involvement, an agreement was struck to bring the house to Salem as part of a cultural exchange. It was carefully dismantled, brought over and reassembled just outside the museum's atrium, opening to the public in 2003.

Changing exhibits in the museum's large upstairs galleries now embrace works from cutting-edge contemporary Native American and Chinese art to the bucolic scenes of *Painting Summer in New England*. While some are traveling exhibits, many originate with museum staff.

Full-price adult admission is $15. The Peabody Essex Museum (PEM for short) is across the street from the National Park Service Visitor Center and a large parking garage.

161 Essex St., Salem
978-745-9500
www.pem.org

Phillips House

The solid appearance of this Federal-style mansion on history-laden Chestnut Street belies its origins in reality-TV-quality domestic discontent.

The story begins in 1800, when Captain Nathaniel West and his wife Elizabeth built a country estate in South Danvers, a few miles from Salem. Elizabeth was the daughter of millionaire Elias Hasket Derby, one of the kings of Salem's great age of sail, and apparently no fool herself. The marriage ended in a nasty divorce, and when Elizabeth died in 1814, she left the house to their three daughters to keep it out of her ex's hands. However, when their youngest daughter, Sarah, died five years later, Nathaniel inherited a third of the estate.

That was taken to mean four rooms of the Danvers house, *which he had removed and hauled to Salem by oxen.*

Those four rooms make up the front of the Chestnut Street house, which was gradually built up around them. West lived in the home until 1836, when it became a boarding house and school. Over the years the house was sold, added onto and remodeled, until Anna Wheatland Phillips bought the house in 1911. She and her husband, Stephen Willard Phillips, undertook a major renovation in the Colonial Revival style, which left the house essentially as it looks today.

Their son, Stephen Phillips, died in 1971 and requested that his childhood home be turned into a historic museum. His widow opened the Stephen Phillips Memorial Charitable Trust for Historic Preservation in 1973. Historic New England acquired the house in 2006.

Programming and exhibits focus on the Phillips family collections of furnishings, art, and antiques as well as life in Salem in the early twentieth century. Carriages used by the family and three of their cars from that time, including a couple of Pierce Arrows, are on display in the carriage house.

The house is open for guided tours Tuesday through Sunday in season and on weekends only November through May.

34 Chestnut St., Salem
978-744-0440
www.historicnewengland.org

Salem Maritime
National Historic Site

This nearly ten-acre campus does its best to take you back to Salem's heyday as a maritime power. It does so most powerfully with the Friendship, a modern reconstruction of a three-masted Salem East Indiaman.

The original Friendship was built in 1797 nearby in the South River shipyard of Enos Briggs and made fifteen voyages to ports in Europe, India, China, South America, the Caribbean and the Mediterranean before she was captured by the British in September 1812. The National Park Service built the new Friendship in the 1990s, based on a model of the original at the Peabody Essex Museum, along with historical documents. Instead of fragrant cargoes of exotic spice or coffee, the Friendship now boards only those who visit her at Derby Wharf for a dockside tour. The 171-foot ship does sail on special occasions, for maritime festivals and other events.

Aside from the Friendship and a small warehouse, half-mile-long Derby Wharf now looks like a simple stone breakwater, its gravel path well used by joggers, dog walkers and tourists taking in the views of Salem harbor. But it was the bustling heart of Salem's maritime business for decades, including the golden age between the Revolution and the War of 1812, when cargoes from around the world were landed here. Historic photos show the wharf lined with warehouses, sail shops and related business. Salem merchant Richard Derby began building it in 1762, and his son Elias Hasket Derby ran the family's trading empire from the counting house at the head of the wharf. Elias's children expanded it to its present length in the early 1800s. The small working lighthouse at the end dates to 1871.

By the turn of the Twentieth Century, though, the maritime trade was fading or moving elsewhere, and the buildings on the wharf fell into disrepair. In 1937 the wharf was one of several waterfront properties turned over to the National Park Service for preservation as part of the nation's first National Historic Site.

The site includes several historic buildings also connected to the city's maritime trade, notably the Federal-style 1819 Custom House across Derby Street from the wharf. The U.S. Customs Service used the building until the 1930s, and it now features restored rooms and exhibits. It is perhaps best known as the spot where Nathaniel Hawthorne worked rather unhappily from 1846-49, lean years that preceded his writing "The Scarlet Letter."

Warehouses, the Customs Service scale house, and the elegant Georgian home that Richard Derby built for Elias as a wedding present in 1762 are also here.

Educational programs and tours of the different buildings and the Friendship run on varying schedules. Your best bet is to drop in at the orientation center on Derby Street near the wharf and consult with a National Park Ranger. Hours vary slightly with the seasons.

193 Derby St., Salem
(978) 740-1650
www.nps.gov

Salem 1630: Pioneer Village

A re-creation of the English settlement established by Roger Conant and company four years earlier gives insight into the hardships and pleasures of early colonial life. Built in 1930, Pioneer Village calls itself America's first living history museum, beating Plimoth Plantation and Old Sturbridge Village by more than fifteen years.

A short drive from downtown Salem, Pioneer Village covers three acres with re-creations of several types of colonial dwellings, including primitive dugouts, thatched roof cottages and the Governor's Faire House, along with gardens and a blacksmith shop.

In 2008, Gordon College took over management of the museum and Salem's Old Town Hall, leasing them from the city. A college theater group stages historical performances in both.

Pioneer Village is open seasonally for self-guided and guided tours on Fridays, Saturdays and Sundays.

Forest River Park, Salem
978-867-4767
www.pioneervillagesalem.com

Salem Witch Trial Memorial

The exact location of the hangings is uncertain, and many of the executed were denied regular burials. The simple, solemn Salem Witch Trial Memorial, near Charter and Liberty Streets, is where those who wish to remember the victims can come to reflect.

This powerful memorial consists of twenty granite benches jutting from the dry stone wall around three sides of a small park. Each bench is engraved with the name of one of the accused and their fate. Their brave and defiant declarations of innocence are carved into the stone threshold at the entrance to the memorial. Lending a meaningful backdrop to the scene is the adjacent seventeenth-century Charter Street Burying Point.

Creators James Cutler and Maggie Smith were inspired by the Vietnam Memorial in Washington. Elie Wiesel was among those who spoke at the memorial's dedication, as part of the 300th anniversary commemorations of the witch trials in 1992. That year also saw the awarding of the first annual Salem Award for Human Rights and Social Justice.

The Salem Award Foundation raised funds for a needed restoration of the memorial, which was rededicated in September 2012.

Liberty Street, Salem
www.salemaward.org

Salem Witch Museum

Opened in 1972, not long after "Bewitched" put occult Salem on tourists' radar, the Salem Witch Museum is the longest-running and busiest of the city's many commercial witch-related attractions.

Visitors enter the museum, ironically enough a former church, and sit on benches around the sides. The lights go down, and a recorded voice-over narrates a series of spot-lit tableaux telling the story of 1692. These are life-size dioramas, with no moving parts. In short, this is an old-fashioned, low-tech show, and some will say it could use updating. But it is also faithful to the harsh facts of the tale, which gives it a certain gravity and puts it above many of the wax museums and spook shows around town.

With its cloak and spooky hat, the statue in the square in front of the museum is often assumed to depict a witch-trial figure. But it's actually Salem founder Roger Conant.

Full price adult admission is $9. Tickets are timed to performances, and this is a popular attraction with bus tours and other groups. Across the street from Salem Common and near the Hawthorne Hotel, the museum is open daily year-round, except for major holidays.

19½ Washington Square North, Salem
978-744-1692
www.salemwitchmuseum.com

Witch House

The only standing structure in Salem directly connected to the events of 1692 is the steep-gabled home that belonged to Judge Jonathan Corwin.

Corwin bought the house in 1675, when he was 24, and lived there for more than forty years, including the time he served on the court that sent nineteen people to the gallows.

Response to threatened demolition of the house in the 1940s is credited with beginning a new era of preservation in Salem. Funds were raised to return the home to the way it would have looked in Corwin's time, both inside and out, including restoring the original roof line. It was also moved a short distance to accommodate a street widening.

Guided tours offer insight into the dark days of the witch trials as well as general information on seventeenth-century life. Period furnishings and décor are not original to the house, however. The Witch House is open seasonally, May through November.

310 Essex St., Salem
978-744-8815
www.salemweb.com/witchhouse/

Witch tourism and Haunted Happenings

Many witch-related commercial attractions and souvenir stores cluster along the Essex Street pedestrian mall, Liberty Street, Derby Street and Lynde Street. Some err on the side of ghoulish thrills and chills, but others are witch-positive; T-shirts announce the "Witches Protection Program." Visitors often encounter members of the city's Wiccan community, and a number of shops offer Tarot readings and other "supernatural" experiences.

One of the better ways for a first-timer to experience Salem is to ride the Salem Trolley. In business since 1982, this combination shuttle service and guided tour allows you to learn the history while traveling between a dozen or more destinations in town. There are numerous other tour offerings, especially in season, some featuring costumed tour guides, and even a Segway tour.

If you visit Salem in October, you'll find yourself in the middle of Haunted Happenings, a monthlong, citywide celebration sponsored by Destination Salem, a public/private tourism group. Everything from haunted harbor cruises to séances to theater performances takes place under the Haunted Happenings umbrella, and many local attractions advertise extended hours. Expect long lines at times as well.

All this culminates with a huge, costumed crowd turning out for the city's Halloween parade. The holiday often brings street revelry by costumed witches, vampires and the like. In recent years there's been a heavy police presence to keep things from becoming too, uh, festive.

Salem Trolley
978-744-5469
www.salemtrolley.com

Haunted Happenings
www.hauntedhappenings.org

5/BEVERLY

Beverly was originally part of Salem in the Naumkeg territory settled by Roger Conant in 1626, but within a few decades was incorporated as a separate community named after Beverley in Yorkshire, England. It has a significant industrial history, including as the home of the first large cotton mill in the U.S. in 1787. The opening of the giant United Shoe Machinery Corporation factory in 1902, which attracted numerous immigrants to town for jobs, was a major factor in shaping the community.

The harbor city also claims a share of U.S. maritime history. The Hannah, the first ship commissioned into the U.S. military by George Washington, was outfitted here in 1775 before sailing, even though its captain and most of its crew were from Marblehead. Beverly long disputed Marblehead's claim as birthplace as the U.S. Navy. (They're not the only towns to make the claim, either.)

These days, Beverly attracts many visitors to its cultural sites, including the North Shore Music Theatre, a large commercial summer theater just north of Route 128, and the Montserrat College of Art downtown, which often hosts gallery shows and other events. The Cabot Street corridor near the college includes the Cabot Street Cinema Theatre, home of the long-running Le Grand David family magic show, now on hiatus, as well as restaurants and coffee shops.

Two seaside hamlets within Beverly's borders have their own well-known identities. Beverly Farms and Prides Crossing are both associated with wealthy summer residents who built homes here in the late 1800s and early 1900s. The original 1906 Beverly Hills housing development in California was named in homage to Beverly Farms by a former resident. Author John Updike lived in Beverly Farms for many years before his death in 2009. Adjacent Prides Crossing is best known to a certain generation of New Englanders as the home of the combative newspaper publisher and conservative firebrand William Loeb from 1955 until his death in 1981. The land along the coast is still home to wealthy residents who value their privacy. But in recent years more middle-class residents have settled inland areas, many commuting to Boston jobs from the local rail stations.

Byway route: *From the Veterans Memorial Bridge, follow Route 1A a short distance up the hill till it meets Route 127. Turn right on Route 127 and follow that through Prides Crossing and Beverly Farms into Manchester-by-the-Sea.*

Beverly Conservation Area

This 126-acre wooded preserve managed by Essex County Greenbelt is known locally as the Beverly Commons, harking back to the days when it was a common pasture for livestock. In 1692, it be-came known as Witches' Woods, as suspect families hid out there.

The trail system offers opportunities for hiking, mountain bik-ing and bird-watching, as well as snowshoeing and cross-country ski-ing in winter. Wooded uplands, wetlands and vernal pools attract numerous species of birds and wildlife, and flora include lady slipper and jack-in-the-pulpit.

The town is the largest landowner here, although the trail sys-tem also touches private properties. Greenbelt conserves the natural setting and maintains the trail system under conservation restrictions and easements. Consult the website for directions and a trail map.

Greenwood Avenue, Beverly

www.ecga.org

Beverly Historical Society

The Beverly Historical Society counts nearly a million artifacts and documents in its collection. Its headquarters is the Georgian-style 1781 John Cabot House, said to be the first brick residence in the city. The prominent ship owner lived there until 1802, when the building became the headquarters of the Beverly Bank. A subsequent owner bequeathed the house to the society in 1891.

The society displays period furniture and décor in several rooms of the Cabot House and hosts rotating community-history exhibits on two floors. The house is open for tours and use of the research library Tuesday through Saturday. There is also a gift shop with a variety of books and other items.

The society also owns the 1636 Balch House, built by John Balch and his wife Margaret, who were part of the original group sent to New England by the Dorchester Company to establish a fishing concern. The house remained in the Balch family until 1916, and was donated to the society in 1936. The Balch House is open Tuesday through Saturday in season. Tours have long been given by a Balch descendant.

The society's third property is the Rev. John Hale Farm, the original portion of which was built in 1694, two years after the Beverly pastor played a role in the Salem Witch trials. He supported the persecution initially and was present at the interrogation of some of the accused. But when his second wife, Sarah Noyes Hale, was accused of witchcraft later that year, he apparently began to reconsider. A book he wrote in 1697 questioning the rationale for the prosecutions, *A Modest Enquiry into the Nature of Witchcraft*, was published in 1702, two years after his death. The property stayed in his family until 1937, when it was sold to the society. The Hale Farm is open to visitors seasonally on Saturdays and sometimes on Fridays as well.

Admission to all three properties is generally $5 for adults and free to society members.

117 Cabot St., Beverly
978-922-1186
www.beverlyhistory.org

Long Hill

Ellery Sedgwick edited the Atlantic Monthly from 1909 to 1938 and owned the magazine for roughly the same period. His other legacy is Long Hill, his family's summer retreat in Beverly. Sedgwick bought the property, previously a working farm, in 1916 and summered there until his death in 1960.

The brick federal-style mansion he built dates to 1925. The interior re-creates – and uses the actual woodwork reclaimed from – an abandoned mansion in Charleston, South Carolina. The decorative motifs include gardens and flowers, but the real ones outshine the architecture here.

Sedgwick's first wife, Mabel Cabot Sedgwick, designed formal gardens and amenities that segmented five acres around the house into distinctive outdoor "rooms." After Mabel's death, Sedgwick married rare plants specialist Marjorie Russell Sedgwick, who added many new and often unusual species to the gardens. The property also included woods, meadows and an apple orchard.

Sedgwick descendants gave the estate to the Trustees of Reservations in 1979. They have not only kept up the property but done much to make it a horticultural destination.

The Sedgwick Garden Library contains an extensive collection of horticultural periodicals and books and is open to the public by appointment. The Long Hill Horticulture Center offers workshops for garden clubs and individuals, in-depth garden tours, and other programs for adults, children, and families. The property includes a two-acre organic vegetable farm run by The Food Project as a Community Supported Agriculture project.

Long Hill is open to the public year-round. Guided garden tours are offered spring, summer and fall, with peak bloom in May and June. There are four and a half miles of trails, including a popular mile-long main loop trail that offers families a way to see the woods that cover much of the rest of the property.

572 Essex St., Beverly
978-921-1944
www.thetrustees.org

Lynch Park

The stories behind this beautiful 16-acre waterfront site, formally known as David S. Lynch Memorial Park, will give you plenty to think about as you stroll the formal Italian garden and take in the view from the seawall.

Initially this area was Woodbury Point, known as the site of an important artillery battery during the Revolutionary War. It had become part of the Evans estate by the beginning of the 20th century. In 1909 and 1910, President William Howard Taft leased the Stetson cottage on the estate as his summer White House. The cottage was directly opposite the main house, Dawson Hall, where Robert Dawson Evans and his wife, Marie Antoinette Evans, spent their summers.

Mr. Evans died in July 1909, just before the president arrived, of injuries sustained falling from a horse. The hubbub of Secret Service agents, souvenir hunters and assorted gawkers that followed Taft to town so disturbed the widowed Mrs. Evans that by the end of the summer of 1910, she decided enough was enough. She told the president he couldn't rent the cottage anymore because she was going to install an Italian rose garden on the site. The Stetson cottage was moved to Marblehead via barge, and Mrs. Evans had an elaborate sunken garden planted in and around the foundation hole. The president moved his summer White House to Corning Street for 1911 and 1912, losing the election that year to Woodrow Wilson.

A notable feature of the park is the "Falconer" statue that shows an Elizabethan youth releasing a falcon to flight. It is a 1920s replica of the well-known 1875 George Blackall Simonds statue in Central Park, commissioned by Mrs. Evans. Some versions of the story have Mr. Evans growing fond of the original during a New York hospital stay.

The park is named for donor David S. Lynch, a local leather factory owner whose generosity was triggered during a trip to London. There he saw a group of people peering through iron gates into a beautiful garden. *Why not go in?* he asked, and was told that it was a private park that required an admission charge. When he died, in 1942, he left

53

$400,000 for the creation and maintenance of a public park for all of the citizens of Beverly to enjoy for free.

By then the Evans land had passed to the sisters of Mrs. Evans, who in turn had left it to the Beverly hospital, which could not afford to keep it up. The city purchased the land in 1943 and created the park. An annual David S. Lynch Appreciation Day honors his gift.

55 Ober St., Beverly

978-921-6067

www.bevrec.com

6/MANCHESTER-BY-THE-SEA

The first settlers arrived here in 1629 and incorporated their community as Manchester by 1645. Train conductors are sometimes credited for coining the long version of the name in the mid-nineteenth century. Other accounts say it was an attempt to avoid confusion with the other Manchesters dotting the New England landscape. More than a few observers, however, suspected locals were putting on airs. As the town's own website notes, "The usage so irked Dr. Oliver Wendell Holmes that he headed his letters to Manchester friends 'Boston-by-the-Charles.'" Manchester-by-the-Sea at last became the town's official name by act of the state legislature in 1989.

Manchester was originally a fishing village, and at one point it was home to forty sea captains. Lacking a deep-water harbor, though, it was unable to provide mooring to their vessels, which had to drop anchor in Gloucester, Salem or Beverly. Eventually the town became known as a center for cabinet-making, but its real reputation rests on money made elsewhere.

Following the new railroad tracks, the wealthy Boston lawyer, poet and critic Richard Henry Dana Sr. made his summer home here beginning in 1845. Soon Manchester became a destination for Industrial Age millionaires whose many guests included presidents and poets alike.

They built massive summer homes along the rocky shore, with names like The Rocks, Kragsyde and Undercliff. At one point, local builders Roberts and Hoare employed two hundred men. Theater-world figures favored the Masconomo House, the popular hotel run by Junius Booth Jr., actor brother of Lincoln assassin John Wilkes Booth.

Unfortunately, many of these architectural wonders were razed in the years following the crash of 1929, or remodeled and "modernized" beyond recognition. In recent decades, a new appreciation for the architecture has emerged.

Manchester also lost several public buildings to post-World War II renewal efforts, including Town Hall, Horticultural Hall and the train station. But the downtown retains enough character that playwright and filmmaker David Mamet shot most of the exteriors for his comedy "State and Main" here in 1999. Ironically, Manchester was a stand-in for a town in Vermont, so the movie never shows the part of town that is actually by the sea.

Byway route: *Follow Route 127 all the way through town toward Gloucester.*

Agassiz Rock

This 116-acre reservation is devoted to a pair of huge granite boulders, stray glacial leavings known as "erratics." Follow a one-mile loop trail up Beaverdam Hill to where Little Agassiz Rock sits, hardly looking "little." Below, in a small swamp, rests Big Agassiz Rock.

In 1874, students from the Essex Institute named the site to honor Harvard natural history professor Louis Agassiz, who had died the year before. Agassiz first theorized that the rocks that dot New England's landscape were shaped and deposited by glaciers – not the Biblical flood of Noah's time. This Trustees of Reservations site is open daily, sunrise to sunset.

School Street, Manchester-by-the-Sea
978-526-8687
www.thetrustees.org

Coolidge Reservation

One way to get a taste of the experience of owning a seaside mansion is to visit the Ocean Lawn here, the site of three Coolidge family homes over the years. Strolling among grass and trees on this scenic promontory, visitors enjoy ocean breezes and sweeping views that can stretch to the Boston skyline.

Thomas Jefferson Coolidge purchased the site then known as Millet's Neck for $12,000 in 1871 and two years later built a white-clapboard summer "cottage" here. He was the great-grandson and namesake of the third president of the United States.

In 1902-04, Thomas Jefferson Coolidge Jr. replaced the house with a brick mansion designed by noted architect Charles McKim, of the famous McKim, Mead and White firm, whose many works included the Boston Public Library. This house was known as the "Marble Palace," due to the use of stone in its design. With its columned portico and elaborate Colonial revival interior, the house received many notable guests, including President Woodrow Wilson. (The Coolidge family also paid for the town library, another McKim design.)

In the 1950s, the Marble Palace was razed by Thomas Jefferson Coolidge III to make room for yet another house, which was in turn razed in 1989, leaving the Ocean Lawn as scenic open space. Over the next few years, the family donated what had become known as Coolidge Point to the Trustees of Reservations, and the reservation was established in 1992. A portion of the estate known as Bungalow Hill, which the family gave to the Essex County Greenbelt Association, was also folded into the reservation, which now encompasses 66 acres.

Bungalow Hill offers sweeping views from glacial rock outcroppings. Birds and wildlife are abundant in the woods and around Clarke's Pond, a primarily freshwater marsh. A mile-long trail takes in all of the these locations, as well as Gray Beach across the Gloucester line, a portion of which is also part of the reservation. The property is open year-round, Friday through Monday, 8 a.m. to sunset.

561 Summer St., Manchester-by-the-Sea
978-526-8687
www.thetrustees.org

Manchester Historical Museum

This local institution includes the Trask House on Union Street and the Seaside No. 1 Firehouse on Central Street.

The white clapboard Trask House was built in 1823 by Abigail Hooper, who ran a successful general store. That same year, she also married Captain Richard Trask, one of Manchester's most successful merchant captains, who commanded the 160-foot St. Petersburg. Permanent exhibits on local history explore Manchester's role in maritime affairs and the heyday of Gilded Age summer "cottages," and include a children's room with a Victorian dollhouse and antique toys. The house also contains a collection of period and locally built furnishings and art. Exhibits are open limited hours Tuesdays through Fridays. House tours are available by appointment. Call for details.

Seaside No. 1 Firehouse was originally built in 1885 to house the town's first horse-drawn fire engine, and it served as the town's police station as late as 1970. It is now home to the Torrent, a hand pumper built in 1832, and Seaside No. 2, a steam pumper acquired in 1902, as well as a collection of vintage public-safety equipment. Seaside No. 1 is open to the public on Saturday afternoons in the summer.

10 Union St., Manchester-by-the-Sea
978-526-7230
www.manchesterbytheseahistorical.org

Singing Beach

This town-owned beach is named for the squeaky, to some musical sound its sand makes when walked upon. Singing Beach has been a popular spot since the 19th century, depicted by innumerable artists. Best known is perhaps Winslow Homer's 1870 painting featuring a well-known rock formation here, *Eagle Head, Manchester, Massachusetts (High Tide)*.

Singing Beach is also known as the only North Shore beach within an easy walk of a commuter rail station. In the summer, as local residents take the train into the city for work, bathing-suit-clad city dwellers arrive by return trip to enjoy a day on the sand.

Along their half-mile-plus walk to or from the beach, they'll pass town-owned Masconomo Park, named for a chief of the Agawam tribe when the area was settled. Benches, picnic tables and a playground make this a grassy respite with a nice harbor view.

If you drive to Singing Beach, however, you will find nonresident parking in short supply. Private parking is sometimes offered nearby, for a price.

119 Beach St., Manchester-by-the-Sea

978-526-7276

www.manchester.ma.us

7/GLOUCESTER

What other community has sacrificed so much in peacetime?
It's said that more than 10,000 Gloucester fishermen have lost their lives at sea over the last four centuries, while building an industry known worldwide long before *The Perfect Storm* hit movie screens. Their sacrifice is honored at the Gloucester Fishermen's Memorial overlooking the harbor from South Stacey Boulevard.

That toll has made the decline of the fishing industry especially painful for this proud community. Government regulation, declining fish stocks and foreign competition have created a perfect storm of their own. Gloucester still has the largest U.S. fishing fleet north of New Bedford, and visitors will always see some of the roughly 250 working boats that port here going in or out of the harbor. In 2010, the catch landed here was worth $57 million, thirteenth in the country. But every year brings new challenges. The city is working hard to diversify the port to support science and innovation, while the sometimes intense debate over development of the waterfront continues.

French explorer Samuel de Champlain stepped ashore in Gloucester Harbor in 1606, meeting some of the native American inhabitants and bearing gifts of knives and biscuits. He christened the site *le beau port* (the beautiful harbor). Perhaps regrettably, the name did not stick, although it now graces the Beauport mansion as well as a locally produced vodka.

In 1623, a group of men from Dorchester, England, arrived and set up a fishing-drying operation at the western edge of the harbor, the first settlement in the Massachusetts Bay Colony. They didn't last, but others came, and in 1642, Gloucester was incorporated and named for the English home port of many of its then-residents. Drying and salting was the only way to preserve cod then, and wharves and fish stages (drying racks) began popping up all around Cape Ann.

Gloucestermen sailed near and far in search of fish. The most perilous job belonged to the dorymen who sailed to fishing grounds on the Grand Banks on large schooners, then put to sea in small dories to trawl for fish. The practice had its heyday after the Civil War and ended by 1930. Powerful draggers took over in the post-war era as families across America feasted on frozen fish sticks and filets from the Gorton's plant on the wharves here.

Along the way, the city absorbed waves of immigrants who came to join the hard-living crews, notably Portugese from the Azores and Sicilians. Ethnic restaurants and festivals remain part of the heartbeat of the community. The annual St. Peter's Fiesta honors the patron saint of fishermen, but it is best known for the legendary greasy pole competition. (Words cannot do it justice – just go to YouTube.)

Geography and culture created numerous discreet neighborhoods and villages set off from downtown, including Annisquam, Lanesville, East Gloucester and wealthy Eastern Point, West Gloucester and Magnolia. Each has their own story. Numerous books have been written about the incredibly rich history of this city – start with the works of the late Joseph E. Garland if you want to know more.

There will be more books written, too, as locals struggle to reconcile the contrasts between the gritty working waterfront and the hip restaurants along Main Street, between rusty trawlers and new "green" maritime businesses. If you chose, you can find symbolism in the Gloucester Harborwalk, debuted in 2012, which uses a smartphone app and numbered markers to help visitors navigate the sometimes mazelike waterfront to historic and cultural sites.

Non-residents are not advised to use the nickname Fishtown, but it would be good to master the local pronunciation of "Glosta."

Byway Route: *Follow Route 127 from the Manchester border through Magnolia to the waterfront and downtown Gloucester.*

At the east end of the harbor, you'll come to a tangle of major intersections. Bear right on East Main Street for Rocky Neck, Eastern Point and the Back Shore. Or take Route 127 straight to Rockport.

From there, Route 127 loops around Cape Ann and brings you back to downtown Gloucester. Return to the west end of the waterfront and take Route 133 through West Gloucester and north into Essex.

Beauport and Eastern Point

Perhaps the most memorable home on the North Shore is perched on the rocky shore of Eastern Point, looking out over Gloucester Harbor. Beauport, the Sleeper-McCann House, was the summer home and personal showcase of interior designer Henry Davis Sleeper, whose clients and friends included Isabella Stewart Gardner, Henry Francis duPont and Joan Crawford. Construction began in 1907 and he moved into the house the next year, but work continued for the rest of his life. With wildly different rooms evoking many different eras and showing off Sleeper's eclectic collections, Beauport is now a museum maintained by Historic New England.

The house began as a modest cottage on land that Boston native Sleeper bought after a local visit. But under Gloucester architect Halfdan M. Hanson, the house's eclectic expansion continued until it totaled more than forty rooms in different styles, including the Book Tower, the Pineapple Room, the Pine Kitchen and the Octagon Room.

Rooms were created, decorated and furnished to evoke significant objects that Sleeper collected, visual themes that he favored, or people and events in his life. The Pembroke Room was created after his mother's death, and featured woodwork from the seventeenth-century Barker House in Pembroke, her ancestral home. The Octagon Room was designed to offer ample display space for tin ware that Sleeper collected while in France with the American Field Service in 1918-19. His many other acquisitions included colored glass, ceramics, folk art and even rolls of eighteenth-century hand-painted Chinese wallpaper discovered still in their crates in a Marblehead attic. All were added to the décor. No surprise that the house drew many visitors, while Sleeper's fame as a designer grew.

After Sleeper's death in 1934, the house was eventually bought by Charles and Helena Woolworth McCann of Oyster Bay, Long Island. Mrs. McCann added her porcelain collection but otherwise left Sleeper's work and collections largely unchanged. Before her death in 1938, she discussed leaving the property to Historic New England, then known as the Society for the Preservation of New England Antiquities. The gift was enacted in 1942, and Beauport has been operated as a museum ever since. It was designated a National Historic Landmark in 2003.

Eastern Point is now a private neighborhood, but accessible to Beauport visitors. The museum is open seasonally, usually June 1-Oct. 15. Full-price adult admission is $10. Visitors receive a guided tour of about 30 rooms, but there are occasional special tours exploring Beauport's hidden "Nooks and Crannies." Tea on the terrace is another popular special event, and visitors are invited to picnic on the grounds.

Before you even enter Eastern Point, you'll see Niles Beach on the right outside the gates. This is a small public beach with an excellent view of Gloucester Harbor. Thomas Niles farmed the point before his heirs sold the land in 1889 to a syndicate that built summer homes. Over the years the point was also home to a Civil War fort, a granite quarry and the 300-room Colonial Arms hotel, which lasted just four years before it was destroyed in a spectacular fire on New Year's Eve 1908.

The current residents of Eastern Point prefer their privacy. However, after visiting Beauport, you'll want to drive a little farther along on the private road and visit Eastern Point Light. A beacon was first established here circa 1829, the current tower built in 1890. The automated lighthouse and other buildings are not open to the public, but there is a small parking lot, and you can walk around the grounds and survey the harbor from the nearly half-mile long Dog Bar Breakwater. Fishermen, artists and picnickers share the views. There is a second beacon, Dog Bar Light, at the end of the granite breakwater.

Look carefully along the shore on the east side of the lighthouse and you'll see rocks that form the profile of a reclining woman looking out to sea, a formation known as Mother Ann. The moaning buoy just off shore is known as "Mother Ann's Cow."

Also served by the parking lot is Mass Audubon's 51-acre Eastern Point Wildlife Sanctuary, which offers shore and harbor views for birders as well as a short woodland trail. The site is open dawn to dusk daily. No pets.

Beauport
75 Eastern Point Blvd., Gloucester
978-283-0800
www.historicnewengland.org

Eastern Point Wildlife Sanctuary
978-887-9264
www.massaudubon.org

Cape Ann Museum

Located near Gloucester City Hall, a couple of blocks uphill from the waterfront, the Cape Ann Museum combines history and art to tell the story of the unique local culture. Everything you need to know about Gloucester's dominant industry is contained in the lined face and weary but resolute expression of Edward H. Potthast's 1900 oil, *Portrait of a Fisherman.*

The museum's collection also includes the largest group of works by maritime painter Fitz Henry Lane, a native whose house is just down the hill, as well as paintings by Gilbert Stuart, Childe Hassam, Marsden Hartley, Winslow Homer, Alfred Wiggin, Milton Avery and many others. Local landscapes, seascapes and coastal views predominate. There are also historical artifacts including Paul Revere silver and an actual redcoat, as well as valuable antique furniture. Changing exhibits often add contemporary works to the mix.

My favorite spot in the museum is actually a first-floor landing where some of the most beautiful works of art on the North Shore co-exist. Soaring over a stairwell is Lanesville sculptor Walker Hancock's study for his monumental Pennsylvania Railroad World War II Memorial. The final work is thirty-nine feet high and lives in the 30th Street Station in Philadelphia; the plaster here, dated 1949-1952, seems majestic enough at twelve feet. Both show the Archangel Michael lifting a soldier out of the inferno of war. On the wall nearby is Charles Hopkinson's large 1914 oil, *H.H. & Her Sister*, a portrait of two of his daughters that seems worthy of Sargent. (It is on long-term loan to the museum from his family.) Hopkinson worked in Boston and Cambridge as a sought-after portraitist, but he lived in nearby Manchester for many years, and often switched to watercolors to capture the feel of the coast. For a time, a nearby alcove displayed his 1957 *Seascape*, which is impressionistic, even sketchlike, and thoroughly modern, painted when he was in his late eighties.

The museum's Fishing and Maritime Collection features historic vessels: the dory Centennial, used by Alfred Johnson in the first solo crossing of the Atlantic Ocean in 1876, and the small Gloucester sloop Great Republic, which Howard Blackburn sailed solo to Portugal in 1901. There is also a large model of Gloucester harbor that explains the workings of fish stages, marine railways and the like. Among the numerous ship models both historic and contemporary, be sure to look for those by Rockport's renowned Erik A. R. Ronnberg Jr.

The museum's Granite Quarrying Collection honors Cape Ann's other industry with tools, artifacts, dramatic photographs and paintings. The museum also houses the largest collection of the work of the Folly Cove Designers textile guild of 1941-69.

Decorative and domestic arts are the focus in the adjoining 1804 Captain Elias Davis House, which offers a glimpse of New England domestic life in the early nineteenth century. The museum also owns the 1710 White Ellery House, located on Washington Street in Gloucester. Both houses are open primarily by appointment.

Researchers and history buffs will be struck by the museum's library and archives, with books, photographs and priceless primary source material such as ships' logs, deeds, maps and genealogy records. (There I once read the testimony of witnesses to a sea monster sighting in Gloucester Harbor in 1817!) The archives are open regular hours and also by appointment.

The Cape Ann Historical Association, which operates the Museum, was founded in 1873 as the Cape Ann Scientific and Literary Association. Its roots go back to the 1830s and the Gloucester Lyceum, which brought to town speakers including Ralph Waldo Emerson, Henry David Thoreau and Oliver Wendell Holmes.

Full price adult admission is $10. The museum usually closes on holidays and during the month of February.

27 Pleasant St., Gloucester

978-283-0455

www.capeannmuseum.org

Dogtown

The strangest place on the Byway. The rocky patch of land high in the center of Cape Ann belongs mostly to the City of Gloucester now, and much of its 3,000-plus acres of scrub forest are protected conservation land. The abandoned settlement's mournful history and unique atmosphere still fascinate, however.

The late Harry Chapin's 1972 song "Dogtown" gets a key fact wrong – Gloucester was never a whaling town – but powerfully captures the isolation of a Dogtown widow amid "the silence of the granite and the screeching of the gulls." Go for a stroll here in the offseason, when the wind rustles the leaves and no one else is around, and you'll feel its strangeness for yourself.

The area now called Dogtown was first settled in the early 1700s and peaked as a small farming community called the Commons Settlement a few decades later. In those perilous times, its isolation seemed an asset. But as the center of activity in the area moved down to Gloucester harbor, Dogtown died out. By the early 1800s, only a few residents remained, outcasts such as war widows, freed slaves and "witches." By most accounts, the community got its name from the dogs the women kept for protection, or perhaps the feral canine pack that remained when the last residents departed. In any case, by 1830 the settlement was essentially deserted.

An 1896 booklet, "In the heart of Cape Ann, or, The story of Dogtown," by Charles E. Mann, tells colorful tales of some of those late-period residents, based largely on fading memories of commonly told stories. Its accuracy is dubious. Reprints are available in local bookstores, and it can also be found online.

Cellar holes and other remnants of civilization still are seen along the web of dirt paths and abandoned roads crossing what is officially called Dogtown Commons. But aside from two reservoirs and Johnson's Quarry, a relic of Cape Ann's granite industry, the area remains largely undeveloped.

Two well-reviewed recent books focus on Dogtown stories. Anita Diamant's novel *The Last Days of Dogtown* explores the hardships of the settlement's final era through characters inspired by Mann's tales, while Elyssa East's *Dogtown: Death and Enchantment in a New England Ghost Town* focuses on more recent history.

Many artists have been fascinated by Dogtown. During the Depression, landowner and millionaire Roger Babson hired stonecutters to carve inspirational mottos ("Never try, never win") into two dozen large rocks scattered through the woods, creating a sort of public art exhibit now known as Babson's Boulders. Marsden Hartley painted Dogtown landscapes that first attracted East's attention to the area, and Gloucester poet Charles Olson found inspiration here.

In the latter part of the 20th century, these same woods hosted teenagers' beer parties and homeless camps. The 1984 murder of a schoolteacher cast a shadow over Dogtown, a story examined in detail in East's book. But in recent years, thanks in part to increased enforcement, most of those passing through are joggers, mountain bikers and bird-watchers.

Dogtown has no visitor's center or phone number. Look for *The Dogtown Guide* at local bookstores, or Google for a map of Babson's Boulders. There is even an iPad app called *Exploring Dogtown*. Maps are also available at the trailhead.

You may still get lost.

Get to Dogtown from the Grant Circle rotary on Route 128. Take the turnoff for Washington Street (Route 127) North. Follow that north a short distance until you cross Mill Pond, turn right on Reynard Street and then left onto Cherry Street. Dogtown Road is a right turn off Cherry. Look for the Essex Heritage sign.

There is limited parking.

Fitz Henry Lane House

Painter Fitz Henry Lane was born in Gloucester and became its greatest native artist, rendering ships at sea and local shores in the clear light of a style later christened Luminism. Lane's granite home on a rise above the Harbor Loop remains a distinctive local landmark.

The son of a sail-maker, he was born Nathaniel Rogers Lane in Gloucester in 1804 and, for reasons that remain obscure, changed his name legally to Fitz Henry Lane in 1932. In an odd, unexplained turn of events, history somehow came to know him as Fitz Hugh Lane, a mistake that was not discovered until 2004, requiring changes to many signs, brochures, museum wall texts and the like.

Lane's legs were paralyzed at around age two – the cause is generally believed to be polio – and he used crutches to get around. He eventually found a love for drawing and developed this talent as the employee of a lithography shop in Boston. He was already a recognized artist when he returned to Gloucester for good circa 1848.

Lane supervised construction of his home on the highest spot of what was then a raffish waterfront neighborhood called Duncan's Point. Its stone construction and steep gables give it a rather ominous Gothic appearance. Academic and critic John Wilmerding wrote that the house's "picturesque isolation" reflected the "quiet loneliness" of the painter, who never married.

Despite the crutches, Lane located his studio on the third floor so he could paint harbor scenes from the windows. He moved in early in 1850 and made his home there for the rest of his life. It was during this period that he became perhaps America's most renowned maritime painter. His style was said to be influenced by his trips to the coast of

Maine, but his best-known works depict local sites, including Brace's Rock on Eastern Point.

Lane died in 1865 and was buried in Oak Grove Cemetery. The house was bought by a neighbor and later briefly served as the town jail, becoming known as the "Old Stone Jug." When the tenements and other buildings of Duncan's Point were torn down in the 20th century, the city saved Lane's house. It became part of a park in the 1960s.

Apparently nothing remains of the house's original interior, and no tours are offered at this time. The house is used for offices and storage by the non-profit organization restoring a Gloucester fishing schooner, the Adventure. It's still worth a stroll around the outside, where besides the house and the harbor views you will see a statue of Lane at work by Alfred Duca. Then perhaps you can walk up the street to the Cape Ann Museum and spend some time looking at his art.

25 Harbor Loop, Gloucester

Gloucester Fishermen's Memorial

English sculptor Leonard F. Craske won a competition to design this monument overlooking Gloucester Harbor. The bronze statue, also known as "Man at the Wheel," depicts a fisherman in foul-weather oilskins bracing himself on a sloping deck as he holds the wheel of his ship. An inscription taken from Psalm 107 is inscribed on the local-granite base: *They That Go Down To The Sea In Ships* 1623-1923.

Dedicated in 1925, the city-owned statue is the best-known symbol of Gloucester's heritage. On the plaza around it are plaques bearing the names of more than 5,300 men identified as lost at sea in service of Gloucester's fishing industry. An annual memorial service at the site, once a local tradition, has been revived in recent years.

Nearby is the Gloucester Fishermen's Wives Memorial, a bronze by local sculptor Morgan Faulds Pike, honoring the women and children who wait on shore "for their faith, diligence, and fortitude." It was unveiled in 2001.

Opposite 57-59 S. Stacey Blvd., Gloucester

Gloucester Stage

The Gloucester Stage Company brings high-quality drama and comedy to Cape Ann each summer, in an East Gloucester theater close to the Rocky Neck Art Colony.

Gloucester Stage was founded in 1979 by Geoff Richon, Denny Blodgett and playwright Israel Horovitz. With Horovitz as founding artistic director, the company performed at the historic Blackburn Tavern in downtown Gloucester.

In 1987, Gorton's seafood company offered use of a building in East Gloucester, which the troupe purchased in 2004 as a permanent home. Given its size and location, the non-profit troupe has had an outsized impact, premiering new works and transferring productions to New York.

The internationally known Horovitz has written extensively about Gloucester and often debuts his plays here, as well as directing. He also wrote the script for the 1982 film *Author! Author!* – starring Al Pacino as a neurotic playwright – which shot briefly in Gloucester.

Horovitz continues to be involved with the company and maintains a home nearby, although he stepped down as artistic director in 2006.

267 East Main St., Gloucester
978-281-4433
www.gloucesterstage.com.

Good Harbor Beach and the Back Shore

One of the nicest beaches and one of the nicest drives on the North Shore. Put 'em together and...

You can of course drive straight to Good Harbor, by getting on Route 127 toward Rockport and turning right at the supermarket, then following the signs. But you'll enjoy yourself more if you wend your way through East Gloucester to the gates of Eastern Point, then head up Farrington Avenue over the hill to the ocean side, known as the Back Shore.

I always think of Monterey, California, and the 17-Mile Drive when I'm here, rolling northward along Atlantic Road on the beautiful stretch overlooking Bass Rocks. The route also offers a fine view of Thacher Island, plus birds and bird watchers, lobstermen at work, sailboats, maybe a seal or two. The only bad part of this drive is the serious case of real estate envy that afflicts many visitors. There are a handful of inns with ocean views, where you can at least pretend.

A short distance north, at Bass Avenue, Atlantic Road turns into Thatcher Road/Route 127A. Follow that as it curves around a reach of salt marsh, and you'll find the entrance to Good Harbor Beach. This is a wide, lovely and very popular ocean beach maintained by the City of Gloucester. On a hot summer day, get here early if you expect to get one of the (relatively expensive, in season) parking places. There are bathrooms, showers and a snack bar.

Not much farther up Route 127A is Long Beach, another nice Atlantic-facing stretch of sand, which is split between Rockport and Gloucester and has perhaps the best view of Thacher Island. There are a few small parking lots nearby, or you can park with a seasonal sticker at the Rockport end. There are fewer amenities here than at Good Harbor, but there is a nice ice cream stand a short walk from the south end of the beach.

Hammond Castle

Inventor John Hays Hammond, Jr. (1888-1965) held more than 400 patents and was known as the father of the remote control. But when he wanted to build a house as a wedding present for his wife, Irene Fenton Hammond, he decided on a historic castle that would provide a suitable home for his eclectic collections of Roman, medieval, and Renaissance art and artifacts.

The vast structure built in 1926-29 sits dramatically on the rocky shore just west of Gloucester Harbor, in the city's Magnolia section. While much of it was built of local stone, there are portions of actual European castles, churches and other buildings that were shipped over and added to the design. This is not a carefully curated architectural reconstruction of anything in particular, but rather an entertaining hodgepodge of periods and styles. (Hammond's father's nearby house, also imposing, is sometimes mistaken for the castle.)

Hammond opened part of the castle for tours when he lived here. It has been a museum since 1973, with tourists and busloads of schoolchildren enjoying the gallery of inventions, the secret passageway and the solarium where Hammond made artificial rain fall.

The great hall contains a massive organ designed by Hammond himself that includes more than 8,000 pipes. The instrument was used for concerts and recordings by organist Virgil Fox, who owned the castle briefly. (There's no connection to the popular Hammond electronic organs favored by jazz and pop musicians.)

Upkeep of aging systems designed by the quirky inventor is expensive and difficult. Unfortunately, the organ is not currently playable, and the artificial rain no longer works, either.

Hammond reportedly engaged in séances and other occult investigations, so naturally the castle is said to be haunted. The museum hosts a popular Halloween haunted house.

Hammond Castle is open seasonally on a varying schedule. Regular adult admission is $10. In addition to daytime tours, there are sometimes candlelight tours one evening a week.

Due to the architecture and stone construction, much of the museum is not handicapped accessible. Consult the website before visiting.

80 Hesperus Ave., Gloucester
978-283-2080
www.hammondcastle.org

Maritime Gloucester

In 2000, nearly 300 Cape Ann residents joined in the creation of a nonprofit organization to buy a neglected one-acre industrial property in the heart of Gloucester Harbor, which included the oldest continuously operated marine railway in the country and several run-down buildings.

Soon the site was transformed into a working waterfront museum with a special focus on teaching young people and visitors about the city's maritime heritage and marine science. The Gloucester Maritime Heritage Center opened its doors in 2002 and has operated here ever since.

Now, like Gloucester as a whole, it is focusing on the future as well as the past. Part of that transition was the new name chosen in 2011.

Maritime Gloucester attracts visitors with a mix of contemporary science and historical exhibits. In the hands-on marine lab, you might find students dissecting a fish or getting to know various sea creatures in the touch tanks.

The interactive Stellwagen Bank exhibit educates guests on the ecology of the fishing grounds off the coast. Exhibits in the Gorton's Seafood Gallery explore the history of the fishing industry and preservation of the environment.

More old-timey sights include the Burnham Brothers Marine Railway, which has been hauling vessels out of the water for repairs since 1850, and regular dory-building projects on site. The Diving Locker exhibit in the basement houses one man's astonishing collection of diving suits and helmets.

Maritime Gloucester has also rebuilt its main pier as the launch site for scenic and environmental cruises. The 50-foot schooner Ardelle, built in nearby Essex by owner Harold Burnham, takes visitors on regular sails and charters in season for an additional charge.

Trips aboard a working lobster boat, the Western Edge, are also offered. The pier even began hosting concerts and parties this year.

Full-price adult admission is $8. The center has traditionally closed in the winter, but that too may soon change, one of many exciting developments predicted.

23 Harbor Loop, Gloucester
978-281-0470
www.maritimegloucester.org

The Perfect Storm

On Oct. 30, 1991, the Northeast was hit by a powerful storm that caused heavy damage along the coast and threatened many vessels at sea. The storm evolved as a "perfect" convergence of meteorological elements, notably the remnants of Hurricane Grace. Among the vessels caught in its vortex was a 70-foot swordfishing boat out of Gloucester, the Andrea Gail, with six men aboard: Capt. Billy Tyne and crewmen Bobby Shatford, David Sullivan, Dale Murphy, Michael Moran and Alfred Pierre. The first three were locals. On their way back from the Grand Banks off Newfoundland, they reported facing gale-force winds and enormous seas. They were never heard from again, despite a massive search by authorities, and only an emergency beacon and a few items of debris from the Andrea Gail were ever recovered.

Journalist Sebastian Junger worked for years to write *The Perfect Storm*, focusing on the Andrea Gail's crew and the hardships of the fishing life, as well as others caught in the storm. Although he could only conjecture at the final hours of the Andrea Gail, the book became a bestseller. George Clooney played Tyne in the inevitable movie adaptation, with Boston-bred Mark Wahlberg as Shatford.

Portions of the film were shot in Gloucester over several weeks the summer of 1999. The Crow's Nest, a gritty waterfront tavern where members of both the Andrea Gail's crew and the movie's cast hung out, is largely unchanged (*www.crowsnestgloucester.com*). The bar is at 334 Main St., a short walk from the dockside location it appears to have in the movie. Staff and patrons may or may not be in the mood to talk about the movie.

At least one character in the film wears gear from Cape Pond Ice Co., which has been helping local fishermen keep their catch fresh since 1848. Tours of the company, at 104 Commercial St. on the waterfront, are available seasonally (*www.capepondice.com*).

The movie's climactic scenes literalized speculation about the Andrea Gail's end, showing the ship overwhelmed by a giant wave. The depiction of an imagined Gloucester tragedy about which the true facts will never be known leaves an odd taste for some, despite the film's fealty to local traditions. For better or for worse, the book and movie shaped the world's view of Gloucester fishermen.

The crew members' names are on the roll of the dead at the Gloucester Fishermen's Memorial.

Ravenswood Park

A peaceful rural oasis maintained by the Trustees of Reservations. Some ten miles of paths and trails crisscross the wooded 600-acre park, which is open sunrise to sunset, year-round. Wealthy merchant Samuel E. Sawyer had summered here and established the park via his will in 1889. It's named after the castle in Sir Walter Scott's *The Bride of Lammermoor*. The Trustees took possession in 1993.

The park also includes a marker where self-described hermit Mason A. Walton built his cabin in 1884. Walton established himself as something of an authority on local flora and fauna and published several books, ironically drawing many visitors to the park. The park now offers The Hermit's Haven Quest, a treasure hunt using a map available at the park entrance or downloadable from the website.

Picnicking, hiking, bird-watching and just unwinding are primary activities here, and there's plenty of nature to enjoy from hilltop woods to bogs and vernal ponds. Savor the Gloucester Harbor overlook or follow the boardwalks through the Great Magnolia Swamp. The Ledge Hill Trail offers a two-mile round trip through a landscape of fern-covered boulders. Carriage roads are crushed stone and considered wheelchair accessible.

481 Western Ave. (Route 127), Gloucester
978-526-8687
thetrustees.org

Rocky Neck Art Colony

Winslow Homer, Marsden Hartley and Edward Hopper are just a few of the artists who've been attracted to this spit of land in East Gloucester over the decades. Eventually a group organized a non-profit

75

corporation that hosts residencies, workshops, lectures and the Rocky Neck Art Gallery. The juried, cooperative gallery gives artist members who don't have their own galleries an opportunity to show and sell their work. It is open mid-May to mid-October.

The Rocky Neck Historic Art Trail takes you to twelve sites of art-historic significance, including teacher Hugh Henry Breckenridge's Breckenridge School of Art, overlooking Smith Cove at 49 Rocky Neck Ave., and the subject of Hopper's famous 1923 painting *The Mansard Roof House* at 2 Clarendon St. Also here is the Marsden Hartley studio at 9 Rocky Neck Ave., where he stayed in 1931 and 1934 while painting landscapes of Dogtown. Maps are available on site or online.

Small galleries, shops and open studios, as well as restaurants and surviving harbor-related businesses such as the Gloucester Marine Railways, make Rocky Neck a great place to spend a few hours exploring on foot.

Rocky Neck Art Gallery
53 Rocky Neck Ave., Gloucester
978-282-0917
www.rockyneckartcolony.org

Sargent House Museum

Judith Sargent Murray was born into a Gloucester seafaring family and became a very early advocate of women's equality in America, including education and job opportunities. Her landmark essay "On The Equality of the Sexes" was published in Massachusetts Magazine in 1790.

Murray was an avid writer of plays, essays, poetry and fiction, and also left behind copies of more than 2,000 letters that are still under study. She was first married to Capt. John Stevens, who built the house for her in 1782. After he died, she married Rev. John Murray, the founder of Universalism in America, in 1788. When he was named pastor of the Universalist Society of Boston in 1893, the couple moved.

The house is a classic Georgian mansion, presented as it might have looked in 1790, with its collection of decorative arts and furniture, including pieces by Robert Sheraton. The portrait painter John Singer Sargent was a descendant of the family, and the dining room of the house features blue and white French wallpaper he donated in the early 1920s. His works are also featured in the collection of family portraits that hangs in the museum.

49 Middle St., Gloucester
978-281-2432
www.sargenthouse.org

Stage Fort Park

The site of Gloucester's first European settlement is now a large, grassy waterfront park with grand views of the harbor. If you're looking for a place to picnic or simply nap in the sun during a busy day's travel, this is a prime location.

This is where that group from Dorchester, England, came ashore in 1623 and set up their fish stages. They might be astonished to find softball teams, bikini-wearing beachgoers and rock-climbers on the site now. Over the decades the park has hosted traveling carnivals and other events, including Buffalo Bill's Wild West show.

A large plaque honoring the settlers' arrival was installed in 1907 on the western side of Tablet Rock, the huge boulder that is this park's most distinct feature.

Climbers sometimes attack the rock's sheer faces, but go around to the back of the boulder and rough stone steps will help you ascend to the top. It's worth the climb, although large chunks of the harbor view are blocked by trees in summer.

Better views are from the path along the shore or a nearby promontory where cannons mark the site of the park's namesake fort. The cannons once protected the harbor, but now they overlook lovely Half Moon Beach, a hidden gem.

The somewhat rockier Cressy Beach makes up the park's southern shore.

There's abundant parking, sometimes for a fee. Stage Fort Park is home to Gloucester's seasonal Welcoming Center, which also serves as an official Byway Visitor Center.

Hough Street, Gloucester
978-281-8865

8/ROCKPORT

Ask people around the world to describe a quaint New England harbor, and most will envision a place that looks a lot like Rockport. Everyone recognizes the red fish shack known as Motif #1, but the wharves, moored boats, narrow streets and charming storefronts all contribute to make this Cape Ann village seem quintessential.

Rockport was mainly a fishing community in its early decades and developed a second key industry when local quarries became the source of much of the nation's granite. Numerous large buildings and monuments around the country were built with Cape Ann stone, including Boston's Custom House Tower, but the industry collapsed at the start of the Depression.

Artists began to gather in Rockport in the mid-1800s, drawn by the quality of light, the harbor views and dramatic seascapes. Now culture and tourism have been the town's economic engine for more than half a century.

Jutting out into the harbor from Dock Square, the spit of land called Bearskin Neck remains one of the most popular tourist destinations on the North Shore. But it wasn't always so bucolic. According to local legend, the neck got its name late in the 1600s, when resident Roger Babson saw his young nephew Henry Witham attacked by a bear near the spot. Babson drew the bear's attention, let it follow him into the water and killed it with a knife after a furious struggle. He then spread the bear's skin on the rocks to dry. Witham was said to enjoy recounting the tale in later years. In another version of the story, Babson was the first to encounter the bear and only went into the water to avoid it.

In later, bear-free years, the neck became a gritty neighborhood of fisherman's shacks and harbor-related businesses. Eventually artists turned those shacks into studios, and they were followed by galleries, shops and restaurants that now far outnumber maritime concerns. The rock jetty at the end of the neck offers an excellent vantage on the harbor and the town. Nearby T Wharf is another popular spot for savoring the views.

The many local galleries and the Rockport Chamber Music Festival every summer remain major attractions. The charm of the downtown and harbor have drawn filmmakers with productions including *Mermaids*, *The Next Karate Kid* and ... well, perhaps the less said about that topic the better.

Parking can be difficult at busy times like summer weekends, and a remote lot with shuttle buses is sometimes used to ease congestion. Look for signs as you drive in from Gloucester.

Rockport was long a rarity – a dry harbor town. In the famous "Women's Raid" of 1856, excess rum consumption by male residents led spinster Hannah Jumper and a group of supporters to take hatchets to the town's bottles, casks and barrels of alcoholic beverages. The temperance banner under which they marched is on display at the Sandy Bay Historical Society, which dedicates a room to Jumper. Residents voted down liquor sales for many years after the raid, although some Cape Ann inlets are said to have been used by smugglers during Prohibition.

In 2005, residents voted to allow liquor licenses for local restaurants. It's still best to check when making a reservation if you want to be certain of a glass of wine with dinner.

Byway route: *Take Route 127 from Gloucester. After a few miles, you'll reach an intersection where Route 127 goes left, but follow the signs and bear right on 127A into downtown Rockport. When your visit is complete, take Main Street to Beach Street and drive north* *along the water. Beach Street soon reconnects with Route 127. Follow 127 for a beautiful drive around the northern and western shores of Cape Ann and back to downtown Gloucester.*

Halibut Point State Park

One of the North Shore's most dramatic landscapes, the park sits at the northeastern tip of Cape Ann, on a rocky bluff with an ocean view stretching to the Isles of Shoals and even Maine in good weather. Atop the bluff is a former granite quarry with sheer stone faces surrounding a deep pond. And on the hilltop above the quarry is a 60-foot World War II-era lookout tower.

Quarrying began in the area in the early 1800s, but the heyday of The Babson Farm Quarry here was around the turn of the twentieth century. Stone from Babson Farm was used in the breakwater in Rockport Harbor. Seasonal tours are offered and there's a brochure for a self-guided walking tour of quarry operations. The quarry itself is now filled with water from rain and underlying springs.

The tower and attached building house the park visitor center and a small museum, open seasonally. You can learn about the granite industry or climb to the top of the tower for even better views.

The harsh winds and poor soil at the site mean that the vegetation is mostly scrub rather than mature forest, but wildflowers and birds make trails here worth a walk. In the winter, if you can stand the frigid gusts, many seabirds are visible feeding just offshore.

Halibut Point is actually two parcels, owned separately by the state and the Trustees of Reservations but managed cooperatively. The park itself is open year-round, sunrise to sunset, and parking is $2. The adjacent Sea Rocks park that extends along the shore to the southeast is owned by the City of Gloucester. Trails connect the two.

Gott Avenue, Rockport
978-546-2997
www.mass.gov/dcr
www.thetrustees.org

Motif No. 1

Except perhaps for the Gorton's fisherman in his yellow slicker, there is no more iconic image of the New England coast than this red fishing shack on a granite pier off Bearskin Neck in the middle of Rockport Harbor. It is often said, hyperbolically, to be the most-painted and -photographed building in the world, taken as the symbol of an authentic way of life that still endures in places like Rockport. The truth, of course, is more complex.

Much of that truth is laid out, some for the first time, in the amusing and informative 2011 book *In Search of Motif No. 1: The History of a Fish Shack*, by L.M. Vincent. The author spent many hours poring through old records and newspaper clippings to determine that the shack was built in late 1884 or 1885 by a group of Boston investors and sold to Gloucester fish dealer Walter Wonson in 1892.

The Motif (some locals say "Motive") began as a modest working shack for fishermen and lobstermen, but by the early 1920s it was already a favorite subject for local and visiting artists, including members of the Rockport Art Association. The Motif name first appears on a painting that artist and teacher Lester Hornby entered in a 1924 Art Association show. Other well-known artists to choose it as a subject include Harrison Cady, Aldro T. Hibbard, Anthony Thieme and W. Lester Stevens.

No surprise that the little red building soon became a weapon in the town's battle to win some of the lucrative tourist trade from nearby Gloucester. In a scenario inexplicably overlooked by Hollywood, a 28-foot replica Motif was mounted atop an old bus chassis and driven cross-country at low speed, escorted by the town's motorcycle police officer, to appear as a float in a parade during the 1933 Chicago World's Fair.

As more and more Americans took to the highway themselves in the post-World War II era, many found their way up Route 127 to Rockport. The Motif was immortalized in countless Kodak snapshots and emblazoned on refrigerator magnets, shot glasses and legions of other souvenirs. Fewer serious artists seemed interested in depicting what had become an icon of coastal kitsch.

The old fish shack's final transformation came when it was smashed by huge waves that rolled into the harbor in the famous Blizzard of '78, on Feb. 6-7, 1978. Although a few residents expressed opposition, the community quickly formed a committee to build a replacement Motif and began fund-raising. It's a sign of the simplicity of the 1,000-square-foot structure that the project took only a few months. A ribbon-cutting ceremony was held that November.

The lobster buoys on the side of the new Motif are bolted on to prevent tourists from walking off with them, Vincent writes, and there is some question of whether the current shade of red is quite accurate. But it's worth noting that the Motif is still at work. The ground floor is rented by fishermen for storage, while the upstairs is leased as an office by a local charter captain and serves as an informal gathering spot for harbor regulars.

Paper House

An oddity in a quiet corner of Rockport, worth a brief detour. Elis F. Stenman, an engineer who designed machines that made paper clips, began building his Rockport summer home out of paper as a hobby in 1922, finishing two years later. The house has a traditional shingle roof and wooden structural elements, but the walls are made of newspapers, tens of thousands of them, pressed and varnished. Some are still readable.

Much of the furniture inside is also made of newspapers, tightly rolled and cut to length. Headlines about Charles Lindbergh's transatlantic flight are legible on the writing desk. A clock and a piano were made the usual way but later covered with paper.

The house has been open seasonally for tours at least since the 1940s. Family members maintain it and live next door. Admission is still just $2.

52 Pigeon Hill St., Rockport
978-546-2629
www.paperhouserockport.com

Rockport Art Association

Although there are many commercial and artist-owned galleries here, the largest and most essential such stop is the Main Street campus of the Rockport Art Association. It has about 250 member artists, including photographers, who are selected by a jury process, and 800 more contributors.

One of the oldest such groups active in America, the association was founded in 1921 for both social and business purposes by a group of artists that included Aldro T. Hibbard, in whose studio they met. By 1929, the group had established its permanent home in the Old Tavern building at 12 Main St., originally built in 1787 as a sea captain's house.

This is very much a working gallery, with changing exhibits and showrooms of art for sale. In addition to the rooms of the Old Tavern, the association maintains the large Maddocks barn gallery across a rear courtyard. This handsome beamed space is large enough to have hosted the concerts of the Rockport Chamber Music Festival before the construction of the Shalin Liu Performance Center across the street.

This is one gallery where you can count on finding images of Motif #1, traditional and otherwise. On a recent visit we encountered Thomas Philbrook's "Say Cheese," which depicts Gumby and Pokey admiring their digital snapshot of the red fish shack, like a couple of tourists. The more things change…

12 Main St., Rockport
978-546-6604
www.rockportartassn.org

Sandy Bay Historical Society

Sandy Bay was the original name of Rockport as well as of the coastal indentation that includes its harbor. The group maintains two house museums in town.

The handsome granite Sewall-Scripture House, at 40 King Street, was built in 1832 by Levi Sewall and contains period furnishings and a wide variety of artifacts and exhibits, ship models and his-

84

toric documents, and works by local artists. Curiosities include British cannonballs dug from local gardens and early settler Ebenezer Babson's knife. A children's room exhibits dolls, games and toys from earlier eras, and the house also hosts the society's research library. The museum is open three afternoons a week during the season "and by chance." The library is open 9 a.m. to 1 p.m. on Mondays through the year, except major holidays.

The Old Castle, on Castle Lane, is a saltbox dating to approximately 1712, and may be the oldest building on Cape Ann that is open to the public. It was donated to the Village Improvement Society in 1929, and restored over subsequent years to show what early life was like in the town's Pigeon Cove section. The historical society took over the property in the late 1980s and has raised funds to conserve the property and document its history. The Old Castle is open 2 to 5 p.m. on Saturdays in July and August; parking is on Curtis Street.

For both museums it is perhaps best to call ahead.

40 King St., Rockport
978-546-9533
www.sandybayhistorical.org

Shalin Liu Performance Center

The most exciting new performance venue on the North Shore in many years and one of the best in the Boston area. Don't take my word for it. "In all the decades I've been performing," pianist Leon Fleisher said from the stage, "never have I come across a venue so beautifully and organically integrated into its surroundings."

The 330-seat concert hall in downtown Rockport opened in 2010. It was built by the Rockport Music organization to host the Rockport Chamber Music Festival as well as other events. From the street, its faux-Victorian facade blends inconspicuously with the other buildings on the block. The concert hall inside, however, is entirely different and dramatic.

Epstein Joslin Architects and acoustician Larry Kirkegaard used Douglas fir, American walnut and other materials to create a warm, natural look that evokes the interior of a New England barn or a sailing yacht. The effect is natural and native and sort of Zen, but the acoustics are precisely tuned. The best feature is the enormous glass wall behind the stage, offering a stunning harbor view as a backdrop for the performers.

In addition to the annual chamber music festival in the summer, the venue hosts jazz, pop, classical, folk and world music performances. Opera, theater, films and community events are also on the schedule.

(For acoustical reasons, performers have the option to close off the glass wall with either shutters or curtains. This happens most often when there are amps and monitors onstage.)

Docent tours are offered on Saturdays, June through October. In season the concert hall is sometimes open for viewing at other times, depending on rehearsal schedules. It's best to call ahead. Or better yet, get tickets for a performance and experience this terrific venue in its full glory.

37 Main St., Rockport
978-546-7391
www.rcmf.org

Thacher Island

The image sticks in the mind: Twin lighthouses standing resolute above churning seas, a mile or so off Rockport. That the towers are 124 feet tall, while the rocky island on which they stand covers only 52 acres, adds to the drama. Appropriately, the history of the island begins in earnest with the story of two survivors.

French explorer Samuel de Champlain noted the island's presence in the early 1600s, but it might have remained just another unremarkable dot of land were it not for Anthony and Elizabeth Thacher. The husband and wife were among 23 people, mostly family, who sailed out of Ipswich in August 1635, bound for Marblehead, where Anthony's cousin was to assume leadership of a local parish. They were caught in a hurricane that smashed their small ship on the island's rocky shore, and the Thachers were the only two who escaped drowning. The couple huddled on the island, surviving on meager goods driven ashore from the wreck, as well as a drowned goat, until they were rescued days later. Among the dead were Anthony's four children.

Anthony Thacher was awarded the island as compensation by the Massachusetts General Court. He referred to it, understandably, as Thacher's Woe. It changed hands several times, until in 1771 the Colonial government bought it back as the site for two 45-foot lighthouses, to warn mariners of the dangerous ledge nearby. The present towers, granite on the outside and brick on the inside, were completed in 1861 and appeared on the Rockport town seal beginning in 1888.

Stories of peril and heroism surround the lighthouse keepers on the island over the years and their journeys back and forth to shore, but both lights are now automated. The south light remains an active aid to navigation, maintained by the U.S. Coast Guard. The north light is managed by the Town of Rockport and the non-profit Thacher Island Association.

The southern 30 acres of the island were deeded to the town by the Coast Guard. The remainder of the island is the federal Thacher Island Wildlife Refuge, established by the U.S. Fish and Wildlife Service as a migratory bird habitat. The north tower is within the refuge.

The island also holds several nineteenth-century outbuildings and a small campground.

You can see Thacher Island from shore, but visiting it requires advance planning. One way is to download an application and join the Thacher Island Association. As a member, you can take the association launch over to the island on Saturday mornings (and sometimes other days) during the season. Reservations are required.

Other ways to get to the island? You can hire the private Ocean Reporter launch out of Rockport, or arrive at the island's small boat ramp in your own kayak or dinghy. Anything larger must use one of the three guest moorings offshore, which must also be reserved through the association.

Various other rules apply for camping and visiting, including no fires and no pets. Volunteer keepers remain on the island during the summer season.

Thacher Island Association
PO Box 73, Rockport MA 01966
www.thacherisland.org

Thacher Island National Wildlife Refuge
978-465-5753
www.fws.gov

9/ESSEX

Essex is one of the smaller communities along the Byway, with roughly 3,500 residents, but it played a huge role in establishing the North Shore's historic importance and shaping its image. Essex was a major shipbuilding center from the 1600s into the twentieth century, supplying the fleets of Gloucester and other North Shore ports.

The area was inhabited by members of the Agawam tribe when the first European settlers arrived in the 1630s. Within a few decades, the community had begun to be known for the sturdy ships built by its craftsmen. It was known as the Chebacco Parish of Ipswich until it incorporated on its own in 1819.

Nearly 4,000 vessels were built in Essex over the years. One oft-repeated statistical snapshot: In 1852, there were 15 shipyards on the river, and one in every 28 vessels sailing under the American flag had been built there. But railroads, steamships and diesel-powered fishing boats gradually made wooden sailcraft outmoded. By the mid-twentieth century, the industry was all but finished here. There has been a small resurgence in recent decades.

The community is perhaps best known now as the birthplace of fried clams, drawing crowds to the popular restaurants along Route 133, especially in summer. It is also a hot spot for antiques shopping and eco-tourism, including boat and kayak tours in the Essex River.

Byway route: *Follow Route 133. That's it.*

Cogswell's Grant

American folk art is the draw at this Historic New England property at the end of a quiet side street not far from downtown Essex. Bertram K. and Nina Fletcher Little bought the property in 1937 and undertook a careful restoration. There's little outside to indicate that this is anything but a well-preserved colonial home with a nice view of the Essex River and marshes. But inside…

For more than half a century, the Littles collected a wide variety of country and vernacular art, ranging from paintings and decorative pieces to furniture, rugs and quilts, redware pottery, hunting decoys and weathervanes. Although Nina Little was a well-known authority who published books on the topic, there's a certain whimsicality to the way the many items are arranged. Clearly the couple took great pleasure in their collection. Interestingly, Historic New England has chosen to display the house as it was in the 1980s – when the arrangement was relatively settled – so you'll find a TV in the sitting room.

The farm began as 300 acres granted to John Cogswell in 1636, when he arrived from England with his wife and eight children. Today the property encompasses the 165 acres inherited by Jonathan Cogswell Jr., in 1717. None of the original buildings still stand; the main portion of the farmhouse dates to 1728. The farm was owned by various members of the Boyd family and by prominent Essex shipbuilder Arthur Dana Story before it was purchased by the Littles. Nina Little named it after researching the history.

Bertram Little was the director of Historic New England from 1947 to 1970, and the couple planned for years to donate the beloved family retreat to the organization in a way that would ensure preservation of the entire property. The Littles passed away in 1993, and the property opened to the public in 1998.

Hay, corn and pumpkins are still farmed there today. Full-price adult admission is $10. The house is open seasonally for guided tours, and the grounds are open year-round.

60 Spring St., Essex
978-768-3632
www.historicnewengland.org

Cox Reservation

A beautiful property offering views of the Great Marsh, Choate Island and Crane Beach – not a bad spot for Essex County Greenbelt's headquarters.

The site is properly known as the Allyn Cox Reservation and Clam House Landing. The Greenbelt occupies the 1785 farmhouse and outbuildings on the site, while the land beyond offers a short, easy hike through meadows to solitude at an Essex River overlook.

Muralist Cox is known for his work in the United States Capitol, the State Department and Grant's Tomb. He bought the property in 1940 and summered here for decades before donating the property to the Greenbelt in 1974. A visit in spring 2012 found art and nature still co-existing nicely. A dozen painters were spread out across the fields with their easels – and a dozen beautiful white egrets picked lunch from the river mud at low tide.

Native Americans occupied the land seasonally until European settlers arrived. By 1650 the fields were worked to support the local grammar school. The property had been a working farm for three centuries when it was purchased in 1940 by Cox, best known for his work in the U.S. Capitol.

The barn behind the house, which he used as a studio, is often the site of Greenbelt events. The main property covers 27 acres; Cox's donation also included a four-acre woodlot on nearby Lufkin Street.

There's no question you're in Essex County when you roll across a short stretch of marsh on the dirt driveway – which occasionally floods in a storm surge – and up to the clapboard house and shingled barn on the rise beyond. There is a gravel parking area with a trail map and rules posted nearby.

Birders will find plenty to watch here, and dog-walkers are welcome with leashes. The walk to the river overlook, mostly on a gravel trail, takes no more than 10 minutes.

82 Eastern Ave., Essex
978-768-7241
www.ecga.org

Essex Shipbuilding Museum

The historic marker at the edge of the parking lot tells the story: *In 1668 the town granted the adjacent acre of land "To the inhabitants of Ipswich for a yard to build vessels and to employ workmen for that end."*

Of the 4,000-odd boats built in Essex, most came together at yards near this site. The Essex Shipbuilding Museum occupies the property known for many years as the Story Yard on the bank of the Essex River, where hundreds of wooden craft, large and small, were built over the years.

These ranged from the small Chebacco boats used to fish nearby estuaries in the 1600s and 1700s to massive ocean-going schooners that took Gloucestermen to the Grand Banks for more than a century. Local shipbuilders even made the transition from sail power to diesel in the twentieth century, and their work continued through various ups and downs until the late 1940s, when steel-hulled boats replaced wood.

The museum has two locations – the boatyard by the river, and the Schoolhouse and Burial Ground a short walk away. Most of the museum's archives are housed in the 1835 Schoolhouse, where exhibits outline the local history in words, pictures and artifacts. The town's first burial ground is adjacent.

At the boatyard, visitors will first enter what used to be the Story residence as well as a shipyard office. There's a brief survey of Essex shipbuilding in words and pictures as well as a gift shop, where you can buy, among other things, books written by the late Essex shipbuilder and author Dana Story, including his local favorite about the craft called "Frame Up!" Educational programs in the workshops out back give visitors the chance to make a trunnel or steam a plank – skills essential in classic wooden boat-building.

But the most profound exhibit here may be the boats on site, old and new. You'll find the 1927 Evelina M. Goulart under a shed roof at the rear of the property. Some 90 feet long, she's the only intact example of the large draggers built at the yard in the early twentieth century, but she has had a hard life and will not go to sea again. The museum's flagship, the 1998 Lewis H. Story, a 30-foot Chebacco boat, floats at a nearby dock. The Story represents the museum at local maritime events, such as Gloucester's schooner festival, and takes small groups of museum members out for sails. Other boats in varying condition are often present and work underway.

If the scene on the riverbank seems authentically chaotic at times, there's usually a staff member or volunteer about to answer your questions. Adult admission is $7 with a guided tour, $5 without.

Some descendants of the Essex shipbuilders are still on the job, although their boats' main catch now is tourists rather than cod or mackerel. Just across an inlet from the museum is the H.A. Burnham shipyard, where Harold Burnham carries on the craft that has involved his family since the 1600s. On one side of the inlet or the other, Burnham built the Lewis H. Story, the Fame and the Thomas E. Lannon, all of which now ply North Shore waters. (See page 148 for cruise information.)

Burnham craft are put together in the traditional manner, with steamed planks that are fastened with trunnels (large pegs, or "tree-nails"). Burnham was one of just nine recipients of 2012 NEA National Heritage Fellowships, the nation's highest honor in folk and traditional arts. That's not to say he shuns power tools, however.

In the summer of 2011, Burnham's yard was the site for the launch of the 58-foot pinky schooner Ardelle, which he built and owns. The event drew more than a thousand spectators, and pictures of that dramatic, old-school "Essex side launch" are on display inside the museum (and at the head of this chapter). Burnham now sails the Ardelle out of Maritime Gloucester during the season.

These days Burnham is often busy sailing the Ardelle, but if you see work in progress, a request to come look around will usually be answered in the affirmative. Power tools aside, it's about as close to 1668 as you can get.

66 Main St. Essex
978-768-7541
www.essexshipbuildingmuseum.org

Fried clams

Take a freshly shucked softshell clam, dip it in milk, then in flour. Deep-fry until golden brown. Serve with tartar sauce, French fries and maybe cole slaw. It seems so simple, but there's genius in there somewhere, a combination of tastes and textures that seems inevitable and, well, *awesome.*

Traveling through Essex on Route 133, you're in the holy land of the fried clam.

Lawrence "Chubby" Woodman is widely credited with inventing the dish on July 3, 1916, with bivalves he'd dug himself from the muddy flats of the Essex River close by his family's restaurant. According to the official Woodman's of Essex account, he was looking for something to stimulate business when a fisherman named Tarr suggested dropping a few clams into the deep-fat fryer Woodman used to make potato chips. The result was a big hit with the next day's holiday crowds and has been a staple in Essex and throughout the Northeast pretty much ever since. (As with all such origin stories, there have been competing claims, which we choose to ignore.)

Everyone's version of the recipe is different, employing milk or evaporated milk or buttermilk, flour or corn flour, frying in peanut oil or vegetable oil or lard. Some diners favor cocktail sauce over tartar, or add a lemon wedge. But most everyone agrees that the Ipswich softshell clam – harvested in Ipswich, Essex and Rowley – is the perfect bivalve for the meal.

Woodman's, open year-round at the eastern end of the causeway in downtown Essex, is the most famous fried clam vendor and would not have maintained its devoted clientele without serving good food. Its large, wood-décor dining rooms maintain something of the old-timey clam shack atmosphere, despite the gift shop out back and the out-of-state license plates crowding the parking lot. The restaurant was one of the locations for the 2009 filming of Adam Sandler's *Grown Ups* on the North Shore.

Many fried-clam devotees swear by J.T. Farnham's, on the edge of the marsh a few hundred yards east on Route 133. Open seasonally, Farnham's doesn't have Hollywood credits or a website, but it does have outdoor dining on picnic tables. The view across the marsh includes an osprey nesting platform and an old house that has become the oft-painted Essex equivalent to Motif No. 1.

While the Woodman's-vs.-Farnham's debate is longstanding, recently some reviewers have endorsed the fried clams at Essex Seafood, another short hop east on Route 133. Fried-clam lovers also throng the Clam Box a few miles north in neighboring Ipswich. The Clam Box, opened in 1938, is known far and wide for its novelty architecture, resembling a cardboard takeout carton. This classic roadside attraction was once featured in the *Zippy the Pinhead* comic strip. Whether it's the food or the look, the line here is often out the door.

It should be noted that fried clams are also excellent when slipped into a grilled or toasted hotdog bun to make a clam roll. But most locals will steer clear of anything listed on a menu as "clam strips." While many think these are actually softshell clams with the flavorful belly cut away for the squeamish, usually they are strips cut from the foot of larger, hard-shell clams. Ipswich businessman Thomas Soffron invented the clam strip in the early 1930s because he didn't like clam bellies, but found they were also a more durable product for freezing and shipping. Soffron's business became a success after sealing a deal to sell clam strips to the Howard Johnson's restaurant chain.

Woodman's of Essex, 121 Main St., Essex
978-768-6057
www.woodmans.com

J.T. Farnham's, 88 Eastern Ave., Essex
978-768-6643

Essex Seafood, 143 Eastern Ave, Essex
978-768-7233
www.essexseafood.com

Clam Box of Ipswich, 246 High St, Ipswich
978-356-9707
www.ipswichma.com/clambox

Warren-Weld Woodland

A modest 106-acre Essex County Greenbelt preserve, somewhat off the beaten path.

Walk your dog, bring your binoculars and bird book or simply enjoy an easy hike through this relatively undisturbed woods. Rare creatures like flying squirrels and saw-whet owls are said to live here, and vernal pools host a variety of amphibians. The woodland is part of a corridor used by wildlife to move between the Essex marshes and the Manchester/Essex Woods.

Warren-Weld Woodland is just south of Route 133 and downtown Essex. Take Southern Avenue to Apple Street, which is narrow and twisty. The Woodland is about a half mile in on your left. There is a parking area for a handful of cars.

Apple Street, Essex

www.ecga.org

10/IPSWICH

European settlement here began in 1633 with a group led by John Winthrop Jr. When the community officially incorporated a year later, it was named after the English port city. Other North Shore towns had better deep-water harbors, though, and Ipswich never attained the prosperity of Salem or Newburyport. Perhaps because of that, it has one of the largest remaining stocks of First Period (pre-1725) homes. Most are still lived in, but major structural and decorative elements from two early Ipswich homes are displayed in the new Art of the Americas wing at the Museum of Fine Arts in Boston.

Ipswich's downtown retains an historic feel. The landmark Choate Bridge, first constructed in 1764, is believed to be the oldest double-arched stone bridge in America. It still carries Routes 1A and 133 over the Ipswich River.

As the Industrial Revolution arrived, the river proved an excellent source of power for local textile mills, and the town became known as the nation's largest source of ladies' stockings. Although the mills long ago faded away, many of the sturdy brick buildings left behind have been repurposed as offices.

Ipswich's most notable property remains the former Crane Estate, which contains the historic grandeur of Castle Hill, popular Crane Beach and a swath of the Great Marsh. It is one of the most popular destinations on the North Shore.

In 1968, then-resident John Updike's bestselling novel *Couples* depicted the mix-and-match sexual adventures of residents of a fictional coastal town called Tarbox. Just how much of *Couples* is based on people Updike knew in Ipswich was hotly debated. From 1958 to 1970, Updike lived in one of those First Period homes, the Polly Dole House at 26 East Street, which is said to be much like the one he bestowed on *Couples* characters Roger and Bea Guerin. Still a private residence, it was one of three places in town he lived over the years. For a time, Updike also kept an office in the Caldwell Building by Choate Bridge.

Byway route: *Arrive on Route 133 from Essex, which merges with Route 1A. Follow them through downtown and on north past the Clam Box. When 133 goes left, stay on 1A north into Rowley.*

Appleton Farms

America's oldest continuously operating farm? That's the claim made for this 953-acre cattle, dairy and vegetable farm. Samuel Appleton began farming here in the 1630s, and it stayed in the family until Col. Francis R. Appleton, Jr. and his wife Joan gave it to the Trustees of Reservations in the late twentieth century.

The Trustees maintain cattle on the farm and a community supported agriculture program, in which area residents pre-purchase a share of the vegetables and other crops to be distributed throughout the growing season. Some 300 acres are hayed annually.

This vast property is also home to many non-working forms of nature, with sixteen miles of hiking trails and a wide variety of wildlife, notably grasslands birds including bobolinks and meadowlarks. Horseback riding is allowed on some trails with a permit.

The western portion of the property is a landscape known as the Grass Rides ("ride" is an English term for carriage path), where five paths meet in a clearing featuring a stone pinnacle saved from the demolition of a Harvard College Library.

Route 1A, Ipswich
978-356-5728
www.thetrustees.org

Crane Estate: Castle Hill

Once cherished by Native Americans for the fishing along its shore, the lands at the end of Argilla Road were converted from rough agricultural holdings to a gentleman's farm by J. B. Brown in the late nineteenth century. Chicago industrial magnate Richard T. Crane Jr. began purchasing property here in 1910 and quickly created a grand summer estate. The family donated more than two thousand acres to the Trustees of Reservations over three decades, beginning with Crane's death in 1945.

The most famous part of the property is the 165-acre estate known as Castle Hill. The first home built there for the Cranes was an Italian Renaissance Revival villa said to have displeased Crane's wife, Florence. It was razed and replaced on the same site by a 59-room Stuart-style brick mansion designed by architect David Adler and known as the Great House. Completed in 1928, the house features a 63-foot-long central gallery; a library with ornate woodwork imported from Cassiobury Park in England; and bathroom fixtures of sterling silver and gold plate. Although the original furnishings were not retained, much of the Great House is decorated with period antiques. Other portions are used for offices by the Trustees of Reservations.

No less impressive than the house is the landscaping, especially the Grand Allée created under landscape architect Arthur Shurcliff from 1913-15. Shurcliff had trained under Frederick Law Olmsted, whose sons designed the formal Italian garden. Shurcliff designed a wide lawn sweeping north from the Great House, more than 2,000 feet long and lined with evergreens of varying heights, creating a stately mall sloping down to the sea with northern views. The notch created in the forested hilltop is visible for many miles. The Grand Allée was used for major jazz concerts in the 1960s, and special events are still regularly held here. Shurcliff also designed the formal rose garden on the property.

The Trustees recently concluded a half-million-dollar restoration of the Grand Allée's landscaping, primarily through replacing trees to restore Shurcliff's carefully calibrated effects. Restoration of other areas of the lawn continue.

Of course, Hollywood loves a good mansion. Parts of *The Witches of Eastwick* were shot on location at Castle Hill in 1986. The film version of John Updike's 1984 novel was set in Rhode Island and shot mostly on the South Shore, but the Grand Allée appeared as the back yard of the devilish Daryl Van Horne, played by Jack Nicholson.

Among outbuildings on the estate is the Brown Cottage, built sometime in the nineteenth century. Repeated alterations over the years gave it the appearance of a shingle-style building of the early twentieth century. The cottage was extensively renovated and modernized in recent years and now serves as The Inn at Castle Hill, offering bed and breakfast accommodations.

The Castle Hill grounds are open year-round to the public, from 8 a.m. to sunset, for $5-$8 per car. The Great House is open seasonally for guided tours on select days, and adult non-member admission to the primary house tour is $12. Parts of the estate are often rented for weddings and other special events.

290 Argilla Road, Ipswich
978-356-4351
www.thetrustees.org

Crane Estate: The beach and the wildlife refuge

The Cranes' land donation to the Trustees of Reservations also includes some of the most beautiful open terrain on the North Shore. At Crane Beach, white sand and rolling dunes draw thousands of visitors and local residents alike on hot summer days. A charge of up to $25 per car on peak weekends doesn't keep the parking lots from filling up.

Speaking of cars, scenes in the original *The Thomas Crown Affair* were shot on Crane Beach in 1967, with Steve McQueen taking Faye Dunaway on a wild ride in a dune buggy, a definite environmental no-no today. Management of the estate is vastly more attuned to protecting wildlife and preserving the natural environment. Some areas of the beach may be marked with signs and roped off to protect nesting areas for the endangered piping plover and other birds from April until September. The greenhead fly (see page 117) is a significant pest for a few weeks in midsummer.

In the off-season, this portion of the estate offers relative solitude for those seeking to commune with nature. The 1,234-acre beach includes miles of nature trails and pitch pine forest, part of a larger ecosystem that continues in the adjacent 700-plus-acre Crane Wildlife Refuge. The refuge, which encompasses marsh, islands and fields in the lower Essex River estuary, is part of the Great Marsh (page 116). Especially during the spring and fall migrations, the refuge plays host to an astonishing variety of bird species, from tiny shorebirds scampering across sandbars to herons, egrets, osprey and eagles.

The most notable land mass in the refuge is 135-acre Choate Island, site of Choate Farm for three centuries. The 1725 Choate House still stands on the eastern side of the island. The Refuge was established in 1974 as a gift of Miné S. Crane in memory of her husband, Cornelius Crane, and both are buried at the summit of Choate Island. In 1995, the island was used as a location for filming of *The Crucible* with Daniel Day-Lewis and Winona Ryder. Filmmakers constructed a small village with a bleak 1690s look for Arthur Miller's allegory of the Salem witch trials. Day-Lewis spent much extra time on the island getting into the role, helping to build sets and galloping about on horseback.

Many locals still refer to the island by its original moniker, Hog Island. The name may have come from hogs once pastured here, or the proximity of a section of Ipswich once known as Hogtown, or even the island's resemblance to a hog's back. Or perhaps all three. Essex residents approved the Choate name way back in 1887, but it wasn't approved by the U.S. Geological Survey until 1998.

The refuge is open year-round, 8 a.m. to 4 p.m. The island is accessible by private boat or guided tour.

Argilla Road, Ipswich
978-356-4354
www.thetrustees.org

Hall-Haskell House

The "Little Red House" hard by Route 133 is the official Ipswich visitor information center. Records are spotty, but when Mary Hall bought the property in 1819, the current house was in place. Hall ran a general store on the first floor that kept her fed during a difficult period in the local economy. By the 1980s, the house was slated for demolition and an ad hoc citizen group formed to save it. Grants were used to restore the now-town-owned building and protect it from the elements. It is part of Ipswich's South Green District.

The interior of the "humble structure," as the town's website describes it, is used seasonally as a gallery for local artists as well as a visitor center. Here you can rent an audio tour of Ipswich that will guide you to those First Period homes.

36 S. Main St. (Route 1A/133), Ipswich
978-356-8540
www.ipswichma.com

Ipswich Museum

A complex of two house museums that has recently grown to three, each showcasing a different lifestyle from Ipswich's past.

The 1800 Heard House is a magnificent example of Federalist architecture with rooms featuring period furniture, décor and clothing, some of it original to the house, as well as artifacts from China and other destinations in the East that were collected by the very successful trader John Heard. Upstairs, displays focus on topics such as Ipswich through the wars and artifacts from the Ipswich Female Seminary.

The highlight, though, has to be the room showcasing paintings by Ipswich native Arthur Wesley Dow, who taught at the Museum of Fine Arts, the Pratt Institute and Columbia University, founded the Ipswich Summer school of Art, and was a major influence on Georgia O'Keeffe. The museum's Dow collection includes several views of the salt marsh from his nearby studio.

In 1936, the last Heard descendant to live in the house, Alice Leeds, sold the house to the local historical society (forerunner of the museum), with the condition that she be allowed to live there as long as she chose. In 1950 she moved to the Hotel Vendome in Boston.

Just across the street is the 1677 Whipple House, which offers a view into an earlier period of the town's history. This First Period home was built by military officer and businessman Capt. John Whipple. Low ceilings, small windows, period furniture and huge fireplaces make clear that even successful people of the seventeenth century practiced a more ascetic lifestyle than the Heards. The house was moved from its original downtown location to its present site in 1927.

Finally, just completed in 2012, is the replica Alexander Knight House next door, an English-style, one-room house with a thatched roof and a mud-and-daub fireplace. The original was built by the town in 1657 for former innkeeper Knight, who had fallen on hard times, and the replica makes clear the less-than-lavish existence of the ordinary person of his day. It was built by volunteers led by local preservation architect Mathew Cummings.

The museum is open seasonally, with parking on site. Adult admission is $10, $7 for just one house. Call for days and hours.

54 S. Main St. (Route 1A/133), Ipswich
978-356-2811
www.ipswichmuseum.org

Russell Orchards

It's a farm, a bakery, a store, a winery and has animals too. While there are numerous farmstands around the area, this stop on the road to Crane Beach, formerly known as the Goodale Farm, is perhaps the most popular.

Come in the autumn, in particular, and you'll find vast numbers of pumpkins for your carving and pie-making pleasure, fresh cider and cider doughnuts, hay rides, apple-picking and more. The crowds are commensurate with the options; on a sunny, crisp weekend in October, parking can be at a premium.

Other times of year bring wine-tastings, a strawberry festival and more. School groups are a regular presence. The Russells are the third family to operate the farm since it started in 1920, but the 120-acre site has been put under conservation restrictions through the Essex County Greenbelt Association, so it will never be developed. Open seasonally.

143 Argilla Road, Ipswich
978-356-5366
www.russellorchards.com

11/ROWLEY

Located between Ipswich and Newbury, Rowley today is a quiet community of about 5,500.

Rev. Ezekiel Rogers served as pastor at St. Peter's Church, Rowley, in Yorkshire, England, until 1636, when he was suspended for his Puritan religious beliefs. He sailed for the colonies with twenty families, arriving first in Boston Harbor and then in Salem by 1638. The group came north to establish the town of Rowley the next year. The town's original borders included a swath of land all the way to the Merrimack River in the northwest.

Early settlers depended on fishing and shellfishing in the Rowley River and used salt marsh hay for animal feed and home insulation. Much of the area within the town's borders today is salt marsh. Rowley also supplied the region with finished wool, lumber and textiles from various small-scale mills. Some dories and ships were built here.

Downtown Rowley centers on a picturesque common and antique shops. If you leave the Byway, the intersection of Routes 1 and 133 in the western part of town is the center of a busy commercial area and home to the popular Agawam Diner, which has been in business at the site since 1940. Have the pie.

Byway route: *Coming north from Ipswich, you'll find that Route 1A and 133 split at the Rowley town line. Follow Route 1A north through town toward Newbury.*

Platts-Bradstreet House

The home of the Rowley Historical Society dates to 1677 and is one of half a dozen known seventeenth-century homes in town. It features nine-over-six windows with Indian shutters and a large center chimney. The society formed in September 1918 and almost immediately set to preserving the house, which was set for demolition. With encouragement and a pledge of $100 from William Appleton, founder of the Society for the Preservation of New England Antiquities, the group purchased the house for $1,000 and set about restoring it.

Today the Platts-Bradstreet residence is decorated to show life as it was during the house's first half-century or so. The attached barn houses a period tool collection. Most of the artifacts have a Rowley provenance.

The house is open for tours by appointment, and there are also special events such as a two-day Christmas open house.

233 Main St., Rowley
www.rowleyhistory.org

Rough Meadows

This newly opened Mass Audubon sanctuary offers a terrific chance to experience all that the Great Marsh has to offer – and in relative solitude.

Just east of Route 1A between downtown and the Parker River, the roughly 250-acre site includes both upper and lower marsh and wooded uplands, offering a feeding ground for dozens of species of birds and animals. Several trails offer varied routes and terrains. Watch the tide tables, for the route known as the Long Walk floods across at high tide.

Formally known as the Rough Meadows Wildlife Sanctuary, its opening in 2012 followed Audubon's purchase of a key parcel of land and the razing of a barn and outbuildings on the site. The sanctuary also includes several properties belonging to the Essex County Greenbelt, and will be managed cooperatively by the two groups.

The upland areas of the sanctuary will offer a place for the marsh to migrate as sea-level rise attributed to global warming begins to affect its lower elevations, officials say.

The site is accessed via Stackyard and Patmos Roads; follow signs from Route 1A. There are approximately two miles of trails and boardwalks, and a small parking area. No pets.

Patmos Road, Rowley
978-462-9998
www.massaudubon.org

Todd Farm

After forty years in business, the Todd Farm flea market may be what Rowley is best known for these days. The old farmhouse off Route 1A is surrounded by acres of fields that sit empty most of the week, except for stakes and cones marking off an empty grid. But on Sundays from April through October, the property comes alive. As many as 240 flea market vendors can be found hawking an astonishing variety of merchandise, from valuable antiques to interesting ephemera to outright junk. Some also sell local products such as honey and garden plants. And just about everyone is ready to haggle.

Check for exact opening dates. There are also antique and bric-a-brac shops in the house and barn, which are open year-round on weekends.

Main Street/Route 1A, Rowley
978-948-3300
www.toddsfarm.com

12/NEWBURY

Newbury started out as the center of settlement between the Parker and Merrimack Rivers, but saw its importance slowly decline as technology and transportation methods changed and parts of the town split off to become separate, independent communities. Today Newbury is a bucolic country town with many farms and fine old houses and much protected land.

The first European settlers arrived in Newbury in early summer 1635, coming by boat from Ipswich, where they had arrived a year earlier. The group, most of them originally from Wiltshire, England, included Rev. Thomas Parker and Rev. James Noyes. Their main purpose was not in fleeing religious persecution but raising horses, cattle, sheep and hogs. They landed on the north bank of what is now the Parker River, and a commemorative stone marks the spot where Nicholas Noyes, the reverend's brother, became the first to leap ashore.

That group and those that followed established a community centered around the meetinghouse on the Lower Green. Within a few years, they expanded their settlement to the Upper Green, where a pond was dug for watering cattle. A separate parish was established upstream on the Parker River, where waterfalls powered the Dummer Mill, for sawing timber and grinding corn. While that area became known as Byfield, it has remained a part of Newbury.

The town wasn't so lucky with other areas within its borders, however. In 1639 the town petitioned the General Court for control of Plum Island, but legislators divided the island between Newbury, Ipswich and Rowley. The part of Newbury that grew up around the wharves and ferries on the Merrimack River found its interests clashing with those of the rest of town and made a controversial bid for separation that was finally granted in 1764, creating Newburyport. And in 1819, Newbury's West Parish split off to create the town of West Newbury.

Like many North Shore towns, Newbury claims a number of possible firsts, including America's first powder mill, first toll bridge and first shipyard. Limestone was discovered in 1697, and the mortar business prospered for many years. There was also a silver mine off Scotland Road from the 1870s until 1925.

A bequest of property from Gov. William Dummer in 1763 created what is now the oldest boarding school in America. The well-regarded school off Route 1 was long known as Governor Dummer Academy, but the name was changed to The Governor's Academy as of 2006, in the belief that "Dummer" was not a selling point.

Its location on the Parker River means the town is a favorite of recreational boaters, and several marinas are located near the Route 1A bridge, as well as a public boat ramp.

Byway route: *Follow Route 1A north toward Newburyport.*

Coffin House

One of three Historic New England properties in the neighborhood offers a look at New England family life in the seventeenth century and beyond. Tristram Coffin Jr. and his wife Judith moved here from the Lower Green in 1678, and their descendants occupied the house until it was given to the organization in 1929. A number of Coffin family members are buried across the road in the First Parish Burying Ground.

Like the nearby Swett-Ilsley House, the Coffin house was originally built with its main façade facing south to catch the sun's warmth, then re-oriented toward the road with a major addition in 1712. Over the years the Coffin House was expanded various times to accommodate new branches of the family tree under the same roof. In 1785, it was divided into two completely separate residences.

Perhaps the most notable occupant was Joshua Coffin (1792-1864), a schoolteacher who lived in half the house for much of his life. John Greenleaf Whittier was one of his students, and later wrote the poem "To My Old School-Master" for him. Joshua Coffin was also an ardent abolitionist and a founder of the New England Anti-Slavery Society with Newburyport's William Lloyd Garrison in the 1830s.

The house still holds a wide variety of the family's furnishings and appointments. And, just as in 1929, there is no indoor plumbing. The privy behind the house was reconstructed in its original location.

The house is open for guided tours only on the first and third Saturday of each month, from June 1-Oct. 15, or by appointment.

14 High Road, Newbury
978-462-2634
www.historicnewengland.org

Lower Green

History fans should stop here, just north of the bridge that carries Route 1A over the Parker River. Surrounded by early houses, the Lower Green is essentially unchanged from the nineteenth century, making it easy to imagine oneself back into the past. Perhaps that's why residents and preservation groups fought hard to stave off residential development in a field just to the west, raising money to purchase a large piece of property to be held by Essex County Greenbelt.

The lone building on the green is District School Number One, also known as the Lower Green schoolhouse, built in 1877 and used to educate children until 1910. It has been restored by the local Historic Commission, including desks with inkwells and period schoolbooks, and is sometimes open to visitors on weekends in season.

High Road and Newman Road, Newbury
www.newbury375.org

Old Town Hill

A short walk from the Lower Green, this 168-foot glacial drumlin was once the site of a sentry post erected to protect the settlement below from Native American attack, especially in the 1670s, during King Philip's War. Later, cleared land on the hilltop was used to graze cattle and sheep.

Now, the trails through woods and fields here are used mainly by hikers, dogwalkers and the occasional easel-toting painter. Views from the top are spectacular on a clear day, from Plum Island to the Isles of Shoals and even Mount Agamenticus in southern Maine. And you might find yourself sharing the view with a wild turkey, as we did on a recent visit.

Trails in this 531-acre Trustees of Reservations property also take in the flatlands on the western side of the property, with salt marsh, meadow, woods and the Little River. Trail maps are usually available at the parking lot. I should note that of all the research trips taken for this book, the one to Old Town Hill yielded the most ticks. Open year-round, sunrise to sunset.

Newman Road, Newbury
978-526-8687
www.thetrustees.org

Spencer-Peirce-Little Farm

Just off High Road/Route 1A near the Upper Green, this Historic New England site offers both an historic house museum and family-friendly activities that draw in many local residents as well as visitors. The story of its ownership drills down through many layers of the area's history.

Most of the site consists of a 400-acre parcel John Spencer was granted in 1635 as part of the allocation for Newbury's first settlers. After Spencer became a follower of controversial preacher Anne Hutchinson, he fled to England, where he died in 1648. The property was sold to Daniel Peirce Sr., who left it to his son in 1677. Daniel Peirce Jr. was a community and militia leader known as Colonel

111

Peirce. By 1690 he had constructed a large residence at the farm, which was unusual for its time in that it was built of brick and stone rather than wood. Apparently he intended to replicate the sort of English manor house that would have been familiar to his father's generation.

Newburyport merchant and ship owner Nathaniel Tracy bought the farm from the Peirce family in 1778. When he died, in 1796, it was sold to Offin Boardman, who had sailed on Tracy's ships and made a name for himself during the Revolution with his privateering exploits. Boardman added a wing to the main house, as well as a wooden farmhouse that was connected to it by a breezeway and used mainly for servant's quarters. Boardman died in 1811, having lost his wharf in the great Newburyport fire that year and fallen into debt.

By 1861 the farm belonged to farmer and investor Edward Little, whose descendants lived there for more than a century. The property came to Historic New England upon the death of the last family member in 1986.

During much of the twentieth century, the wooden farmhouse was occupied by the family of Jacob Stekionis, who was hired as a farmhand in 1913. His widow, Dorothy, lived there until she died in 1993.

Historic New England spent more than a million dollars and several years stabilizing and preserving the main house. It opened to the public in 1992. Thanks to good property maps resulting from the many sales and transfers, several parts of the site, including Boardman's privy, were excavated and studied extensively by Boston University archaeologists.

What truly brought the Spencer-Peirce-Little Farm close to the heart of locals, though, was the decision to return animals to the farm for the first time in decades in 2004, through a partnership with the Massachusetts Society for the Prevention of Cruelty to Animals. The turkey named Socrates was so popular with local children that when he passed away in 2009, it made the local newspapers. Rescued animals remain a large part of the farm's appeal, with turkeys, sheep, horses and more on premises.

Regular adult admission is $5. The farm hosts numerous community and special events, including a popular old-time baseball series played by rules from the 1800s.

5 Little's Lane, Newbury
978-462-2634
www.historicnewengland.org

Swett-Ilsley House

Adjacent to the Newburyport town line on High Road/Route 1A, this was the first house acquired by Historic New England, back in 1911.

The original portion was built in 1670 by Stephen Swett, and an early addition features a huge brick fireplace, nearly thirteen feet wide with three beehive ovens. Subsequent additions more than doubled the square footage. Sitting on what was for many years the busiest road in town, the structure at various times housed a tavern, chocolate mill, chandlery, tobacco shop and more.

Conservators have stripped away later layers to expose the house's original timbers, paneling and the fireplace. But the house has not been restored or furnished, and is used as a "study museum" where historians and craftsmen can investigate period design and building techniques.

The Swett-Ilsley House is open for guided tours only on the first Saturday of each month, from June to October, or by appointment.

4 High Road, Newbury
978-462-2634
www.historicnewengland.org

13/PLUM ISLAND

Plum Island is a narrow, nine-mile-long barrier island that stretches from the Merrimack River in the north to Ipswich Bay in the south. The island protects portions of the Great Marsh and the mainland from Atlantic Ocean storms. Its ocean side consists of a vast, uninterrupted beach of unimpeachable beauty.

Seasonal and year-round homes are crowded onto the northern third of the island. The Parker River National Wildlife Refuge, known as one of the prime bird-watching spots on the entire East Coast, takes up most of the rest, with dunes, maritime forest and wetlands behind the beach.

It would be easy to say that its natural beauty and independent spirit earned Plum Island its own chapter in this book, but the truth is more mundane. From north to south, sections of the island fall within the borders of Newburyport, Newbury, Rowley and Ipswich. Rather than try to divide the island's attractions among them, I've made it stand on its own.

The island is likely named for the beach plum that grows wild here and is sometimes made into jelly. By the mid-1600s, it already was used as pasture for hogs, horses and cattle. At first, people reached the island by driving horses or wagons across the marsh at low tide, but in 1805 a road was constructed, and a trolley line followed. The island became a popular vacation resort, with hotels and guest houses.

By the middle of the twentieth century, Plum Island had evolved into a working-class getaway, where many area families owned modest cottages or rented for a week's seaside vacation in the summer. In recent years, larger, more expensive homes and year-round living have become common.

There is still only one road from the mainland to the island, the two-lane blacktop called Plum Island Turnpike, which crosses the Plum Island River on the Sgt. Donald Wilkinson Bridge, a drawbridge. Bird-watching opportunities begin here, with cormorants sitting on utility lines and brilliant white egrets standing out (in both senses) on the marsh.

Plum Island is a popular spot for local surfers, although occasionally the water can be rough for swimming. A winter beach walk is one of the great pleasures of living nearby.

Beach parking outside of the refuge is clustered at two locations. Directly ahead as you reach the island is the beach access maintained by the town of Newbury. There is permit parking for residents and a few spots for visitors, as well as several small commercial lots nearby. At the northern tip of the island, Newburyport maintains a large parking lot and restrooms for beachgoers.

Island beaches are also popular spots for fishermen surfcasting for striped bass and other species. The Surfland bait and tackle shop, an island institution since 1960, is a good place to ask where they're biting.

Environmental issues are ever present here. The specter of global warming and rising sea levels looms behind the perpetual debate here over remedies for beach erosion, which has claimed a few homes over the years and threatens more.

Summertime visitors will want to read on for a warning about the greenhead fly.

Byway route: *Coming north on Route 1A through Newbury, your first stoplight will be at Rolfe's Lane. Turn right and follow this to its end, then turn right again on Plum Island Turnpike to the island. You can also reach the turnpike from downtown Newburyport via Water Street.*

The Great Marsh

This massive salt marsh covers roughly 20,000 acres just in Massachusetts. It begins along the Annisquam River in Gloucester and spreads northward across parts of Essex, Ipswich, Rowley, Newbury, Newburyport and Salisbury, continuing into New Hampshire. The Great Marsh is by far the single most ecologically important feature of the North Shore landscape. The creation of the Parker River National Wildlife Refuge was just one of many attempts to protect it.

While it may look flat and dull to the untrained eye, the marsh teems with a matchless biological richness, a diversity of birds, animals, plant and marine life. Its complex natural systems involve several types of environment. Channels and mudflats carry the rise and flow of the tides that maintain its existence. Barrier beaches like Plum Island shelter it from ocean waves.

The marshland itself consists of mud and peat created by the layering of thousands of years of marsh grass. There are two main types of grasses: cordgrass (*spartina alterniflora*) and salt marsh hay (*spartina patens*). Cordgrass grows at the edges of the marsh, where it is inundated by high tides twice a day, while marsh hay tends to be on higher levels that flood only monthly, with the lunar high tides.

Salt marsh hay was important to early settlers, who harvested it for everything from animal bedding and feed to insulation for homes. Cordgrass was used primarily for roof thatch. A little marsh hay is still harvested today. In a few places, rounded haystacks can be seen resting on wooden "staddles" (platforms) in the marsh to keep them dry.

Some say that the geometric ditches seen in places in the marsh were dug by settlers to speed drainage, to aid haying or animal grazing. Such work did occur, but the ditches seen in the marsh now are mostly remnants of mosquito abatement projects undertaken as part of Depression-era job-creation projects. In fact, neither sort of ditch was effective. Man could not improve on the marsh's natural hydrology, and the mosquito projects were actually more harmful to minnows that were the insect's predators.

The marsh's value to wildlife is inestimable. There are always birds to see here, and mammals such as deer, fox and coyotes are common if elusive. The marsh also provides habitat and spawning ground for innumerable maritime species, including the softshell clams, mussels and oysters that are pulled from its mudflats by both commercial and recreational diggers. Local residents are well acquainted with the insect population, particularly the greenhead fly. The saltmarsh dragon is a unique species of dragonfly that lives in the salt pannes.

In spring and late summer the marsh is also a crucial stopover for millions of migratory birds, including ducks, geese, swallows, egrets, and herons, providing a variety of spectacular sights and sounds for visitors. In the winter, snowy owls and other species arrive from the north, sometimes via Boston's Logan Airport, where they are removed from the runways and released on Plum Island.

Despite its value, the marsh was often ignored, treated as wasted land or used as a dumping ground. It wasn't until the ecology movement of the 1960s and beyond that its importance was fully recognized.

As a fragile ecosystem, the marsh faces immediate challenges including diminishing fresh water from local rivers, invasive plants such as phragmites, and development. But the greater threat looms from global warming, which is expected to bring rising sea levels and permanently inundate parts of the marsh. Scientists are already assessing the marsh's reaction and eyeing neighboring uplands where the marsh may migrate as the ocean rises.

Greenhead fly

In the summer, every island visitor needs to know about the bloodthirsty greenhead fly (*Tabanus nigrovittatus*), a type of biting horsefly that is found all around the Great Marsh but seems especially intense on Plum Island and Crane Beach. Greenhead season usually lasts from the beginning of July into August. It's tempting to think of it as an invasion, but of course we're the ones invading their turf.

Greenheads breed in the salt marshes. After laying their first batch of eggs each summer, the females need the nourishment of fresh blood before producing more. They get it from you. Only the females bite, but the bites are painful and can leave a large welt. Many a first-time island visitor has been driven right back to the mainland by their relentless attacks. Commercial insect repellents do not deter them, although some locals say Avon's Skin So Soft bath oil does the trick. It does seem that greenheads like to sleep in, and an early-morning walk or bike ride through their habitat may pass peacefully.

Greenhead traps – black boxes on stands you'll see throughout the marsh – keep a check on their population, which seems to wax and wane from year to year depending on seasonal factors. Popular theory connects their breeding cycle to the moon and tides, but more likely the greenheads' emergence each summer is simply a matter of achieving sufficient degree-days.

Some locals half-seriously credit the greenheads as a factor in preserving the coast from more rapacious development. They can even be inspirational. Painter Sam Holdsworth's eerie and hilarious Greenhead Series depicts the flies as a faceless alien horde in works like *Everybody Waits At Woodman's*, which is in the collection of the Cape Ann Museum. And a distillery in Ipswich offered Greenhead Spiced Rum – for the summer only, naturally – in 2012.

Parker River National Wildlife Refuge

The 4,662-acre Parker River National Wildlife Refuge was established in 1942 to provide feeding, resting, and nesting habitat for migratory birds. Some 3,000 of those acres are part of the Great Marsh.

The remainder is primarily sand dune and scrub forest on Plum Island. This land was once dotted with dozens of family "camps," generally without running water or electricity, which were used for hunting, fishing and beach-going. The federal land-taking to create the refuge after World War II was opposed by many owners and phased in over a number of years. Only one camp remains intact, while occasionally the foundations of others can be seen poking up through the sand.

The refuge offers a permanent home or migratory stop to more than 300 species of birds plus deer, coyote and other animals. But in a circumstance uncommon among federal refuges, the habitat is shared with many humans. A single two-lane roadway snakes down along the marsh side of the island for more than six miles; roughly the first half is paved, and the remainder is dusty gravel. Along the way are a handful of small parking lots offering beach and trail access, as well as live-parking areas for bird-watching along the shallow salt pannes. Lookout towers offer spectacular views.

The refuge beach is closed each spring and summer, in whole or in part, for the protection of a tiny, endangered shorebird called the piping plover. The birds nest in vulnerable areas of the beach, and the closing is intended to protect them until chicks fledge in mid- to late-summer. Unaware beachgoers who find themselves turned away sometimes react with annoyance. Surfcasters and fishermen with drive-on beach permits are also affected, and a few local cars bear faded bumper stickers that say *Plover Tastes Like Chicken*. But many if not most people support the policy, based on the refuge's credo: Wildlife first.

When the beaches are open, the refuge's limited parking often fills up on sunny weekends, leading to long lines outside the gatehouse. But at other times of year, especially in the fall, you can find relative solitude by parking in one of the small lots and walking the boardwalk across the dunes to the refuge beach.

The refuge visitors center is actually on the mainland, in Newburyport, across the street from Mass Audubon's Joppa Flats Education Center. The center offers informative displays and educational programs as well as a gift shop. Refuge passes and permits can be purchased there. For those planning to visit more than a couple of times in a year, an annual pass is usually a good bargain. Refuge admission is $5 per car; bike or hike in for $2 a person.

Note: Absolutely no dogs or other pets are permitted in the refuge, even in your car.

Refuge: Sunset Drive, Plum Island
Visitors Center: 6 Plum Island Turnpike, Newburyport
978-465-5753
www.fws.gov

Plum Island Airport

Like the Refuge Visitors Center, Plum Island Airport (FAA designator B2B) is actually on the mainland side of the marsh, off Plum Island Turnpike at the Newbury/Newburyport line. Operated by the non-profit Plum Island Aerodrome, Inc., it is a working airport that hosts sightseeing flights, flying lessons and events such as historic aircraft fly-ins and model plane rallies.

The modest airport headquarters contains the one-room Burgess Museum, a stop for early-aviation buffs. It turns out that the airport's forerunner, a crude strip just across the marsh on the back side of Plum Island, was part of aviation history.

On February 28, 1910, Marblehead yacht builder W. Starling Burgess and pioneering pilot Augustus M. Herring launched New England's first airplane flight from a frozen lake in Hamilton, with Herring flying a biplane he and Burgess built. By April, Burgess had moved the operation to Plum Island, with a building and wood-plank runway on the edge of the marsh.

Into the summer of that year, Herring and others flew Burgess biplanes over the marsh at speeds reaching – brace yourself – 23 miles per hour. This was such a novelty that the flights were front-page news in the local paper and attracted growing crowds. Many people took the streetcar to Plum Island and walked more than a mile to the site for the show. There were numerous crashes and setbacks, but also successes. Burgess shut down test flights in late summer to prepare for a Boston air show in September. He later went on to build planes for the Wright Brothers in his Marblehead shop.

During that summer of 1910, Burgess even took steps to lease land from the Little family on the mainland side of the marsh for an airplane factory. The factory was never built, but aviation activity at the location began in the 1920s, and the airport has operated at the site ever since. Flying lessons first occurred there in the 1930s, and the airport has been through Civil Air Patrol duties, several changes of operator, and flooding in the Blizzard of '78. The land is leased from Historic New England, which owns and runs the adjacent Spencer-Peirce-Little Farm.

At Parking Lot 2 in the Parker River National Wildlife Refuge, an historic marker gives details and a map showing the location of Burgess's airstrip. The Burgess room at the airport chronicles this history and also includes plane models and other memorabilia.

24 Plum Island Turnpike, Newbury
978-463-4222
www.plumislandaerodrome.org

Plum Island Light

Treacherous currents, powerful tides, shifting sands, thick fog and blustery winds ...

The mouth of the Merrimack River can be quite a challenging passage even today, when boaters are equipped with engines and sonar, while stone jetties and navigational buoys make clear the course. Consider the challenge facing seamen of earlier centuries, who brought their cargo into the river under sail alone. No wonder shipwrecks were common.

At first the only navigational aids available were signal fires built on the beach by hardy locals. But Newburyport's importance in colonial maritime trade meant that ensuring safe navigation of the river mouth was a high priority. The first range lights on Plum Island were built in the 1780s, two small towers with whale oil lamps. They were built on movable bases, due to the frequent realignment of sandbars and channels in the area.

The lighthouses were often moved, repaired and even replaced in coming decades, but frequent wrecks continued, and the bones of lost ships occasionally surface on Plum Island or Salisbury Beach. The U.S. Life Saving Service, a precursor of the Coast Guard, first established a station on Plum Island in 1871. The present lighthouse lit its kerosene lamp for the first time on Sept. 20, 1898. Currently the beacon is a single green, 4000 candle-power light.

After major restoration by the Coast Guard, Plum Island Light was first opened to visitors in the 1990s. Ownership of the lighthouse was turned over to the City of Newburyport in 1993, but it is cared for under lease to the Friends of Plum Island Light. The lighthouse is often open for tours, usually during weekend afternoons in the summer. On a sunny day, the 360-degree view from the top is quite spectacular.

The mouth of the Merrimack continues to challenge boaters, however. Several pleasure craft have collided with the north jetty in recent years, and a barge carrying construction equipment upriver beached on Plum Island in rough seas in December 2002, remaining for several months before being scrapped.

Northern Boulevard, Plum Island
978-462-9802

Sandy Point State Reservation

This 77-acre park on the southern tip of Plum Island can only be accessed through Parker River National Wildlife Refuge. But visitors willing to make the drive, nearly half on dusty gravel, will be rewarded with uncrowded beaches and panoramic views of Cape Ann, Crane Beach and Ipswich Bay. There are only 50 parking spaces here, in two dirt lots, so crowds are small. When the lots are full, access is shut off at the refuge gatehouse.

Surf here tends to be calmer than at the other end of the island, more friendly to swimmers and children. It's also a popular spot for surfcasting. A small wooded hill is generally inaccessible to walkers, but birders will be rewarded for their attention. Sandy Point does not close for the piping plovers, but beachgoers must steer clear of fenced areas that protect their nests. No admission charge.

Via Sunset Drive, Plum Island
617-372-6730
www.mass.gov/dcr

14/NEWBURYPORT

With its picturesque harbor, tourist-friendly downtown and wealth of history, this small city on the Merrimack River is as appealing and prosperous a community as you can find on the Byway. It wasn't always so.

By the early 1960s, once-bustling downtown Newburyport had become an eyesore. The nineteenth-century brick buildings around Market Square stood boarded up and derelict, and the waterfront was a weedy, junk-strewn wasteland. A plan was conceived to bulldoze much of the downtown and replace it with strip malls and parking lots, using federal urban renewal funds. The public display of a model of this "new" Newburyport is often credited with galvanizing support for a different approach.

Visionary local leaders set to winning hearts, minds and wallets for a plan using the downtown's historic character as a draw. The Newburyport Redevelopment Authority spearheaded the effort, purchasing or taking over dilapidated properties and seeking developers for them. A few pioneers invested on their own, renovating buildings and opening shops or offices. The process lasted through the 1970s and beyond, but Newburyport won national acclaim for its downtown revival, complete with parks, a pedestrian mall and a waterfront boardwalk. The sense of possibility also drew a new population of artists and professionals. Now tourists come from the world over to visit New-buryport's shops and restaurants and stroll the waterfront at sunset. The very same area on the south bank of the Merrimack was well known to Europeans by the 1620s, including a disreputable fur trader named Walter Bagnall, known as Great Watt. He was the owner of Watt's Cellar, apparently a storehouse or trading post built into the riverbank near the location of the present Firehouse Center for the Arts. The path identified on early maps as the way to Watt's Cellar is now State Street.

As formal settlement began in the 1630s, the area was desig-nated part of Newbury. Soon there was a regular ferry crossing the Merrimack here. Shipbuilding and maritime commerce became boom-ing economic mainstays, outpacing farming and other trades. Gradually the interests of the increasingly prosperous port residents brought con-flict with the rest of town, and Newburyport set off on its own in 1764.

Entering Newburyport from the east on Route 1A or the west on Route 113, you'll find yourself on High Street, passing block after block of beautifully maintained mansions that testify to fortunes accu-mulated here in the eighteenth and early nineteenth centuries. New-buryport was a political and commercial center as well as maritime power, but shipbuilding, cargo trade and wartime privateering were at the root of its wealth.

Ironically, today's downtown was shaped by a disaster that be-fell the community in 1811. After a dry spell, a strong westerly wind blew up on the evening of March 31. What was widely believed to be an arson fire started in a stable on Inn Street and grew into a great con-flagration. Desperate fire-fighting attempts could not contain roaring, wind-whipped flames or quell oven-like temperatures. More than 250 wooden buildings were destroyed, essentially the entire city center. Many local fortunes were left in ruins as well.

As Newburyport rebuilt, new regulations were put in place, re-quiring the fireproof brick-and-masonry construction that still stands today. Most visitors are enchanted by the blocks of lookalike brick buildings in and around Market Square, with fashionable boutiques, art galleries and restaurants at the street level, and offices or apartments above. Few notice the brick firewalls between the buildings, rising a few feet above the roof line.

The fire combined with the 1807 embargo act and the hardships of the War of 1812 ended the city's greatest period of prosperity. Shipbuilding rose again during the clipper era of the mid- to late-1800s, but Newburyport's economy gradually shifted to manufacturing of products including shoes and silver. In the twentieth century, responding to larger economic trends, those factories closed or departed for warmer climes. As jobs were lost, the local economy suffered, and downtown gradually became a ghost town.

What survived was locals' stubborn pride in their neighborhoods (North End, South End, Joppa) as well as community traditions like high-school athletics. That pride held the seeds of the city's renewal. Now Newburyport has been transformed to a degree that might have astounded even the leaders of its rebirth.

Byway route: *Follow Route 1A north from Newbury, which turns into Newburyport's High Street. The Byway officially ends where High Street does, by Atkinson Common. Along the way, though, it detours off High to loop downtown Newburyport on Green, Merrimack and State Streets.*

A stroll around the waterfront
and Market Square

Whatever else is on your itinerary, be sure you make time to explore Newburyport on foot.

Most people will begin or end their visit along the waterfront boardwalk. In summer the river and docks are busy with sailboats, cabin cruisers and sport-fishing craft, as well as the occasional mega-yacht or historic tall ship. Here you can board a whale watch, a harbor tour or a scenic sailing cruise. Summer concerts are often held on the lawn behind the Firehouse Center for the Arts. At the east end of the boardwalk, by the harbormaster's office, historic markers commemorate fishermen lost at sea and the town's role in the birth of the U.S. Coast

Guard. A handful of commercial fishing boats still unload their catch here year-round.

On a warm evening, nearby Market Square comes alive with shoppers and strollers, people dining at restaurant patios or simply sitting on a bench to enjoy an ice cream cone. Musicians and jugglers entertain, but history is still present. On a wall near the entrance to Inn Street, you can find a plaque marking the local pre-Revolutionary tea party, said to have been held three days before the more famous one in Boston. Another marker, on a Liberty Street wall, tells of an accused witch sentenced to house arrest here years before the unpleasantness in Salem.

Walk east on Water Street and you'll find the Newburyport Art Association galleries, and the shops and restaurants of the Tannery Marketplace. The brick tower of the deactivated Inner Range Light on Water Street now hosts the town's most unusual dining experience and perhaps its most expensive – net proceeds from dinners at the top support a lighthouse restoration group.

Walk up busy State Street or through the Inn Street pedestrian mall, and shops and restaurants abound. The vintage neon sign above the entrance to the historic Fowle's newsstand on State Street – now a restaurant – is a local landmark. There's even an independent arthouse movie theater, the Screening Room.

If the First Religious Society Unitarian church at 26 Pleasant St. is open, it's worth a look inside at the astonishingly simple and tranquil 1801 sanctuary; this was one of the few buildings to survive the 1811 fire. The Paul Revere bell in the steeple is one of two in town. Cell phone equipment hidden in the steeple helps fund the church's upkeep.

Continue west on Pleasant across Green Street and you'll find Brown Square, named for its 1802 donor, local merchant Moses Brown. One of the most successful local businessmen at the time, Brown was a noted philanthropist but also profited indirectly from the slave trade as a major importer of West Indies sugar and molasses. Nearby is a statue of abolitionist William Lloyd Garrison, the locally raised newspaperman who became a firebrand in the national debate over slavery. Educational kiosks tell the stories of the two men. Brown also built the four-story brick building on the southwest corner of the square, now a boutique hotel known as the Garrison Inn.

Atkinson Common

This tranquil oasis marks the western end of stately High Street. Gardens, walkways, a lily pond and a gazebo have served as backdrops to countless weddings, photo shoots, picnics and family celebrations. The park, maintained by the non-profit Belleville Improvement Society, is approximately a five-minute drive from downtown.

Atkinson Common also contains several war monuments and a now-shuttered observation tower built by the Works Progress Administration in the 1930s. At the back of the property are woods and three tennis courts, as well as a path down to the busy baseball diamonds of the Pioneer League Fields on Merrimac Street.

390 High St., Newburyport
978-465-5108
www.atkinsoncommonnewburyport.org

Cushing House Museum

The Historical Society of Old Newbury maintains its headquarters at this elegant 22-room brick Federalist mansion at the corner of High and Fruit streets. The house was built in 1808 for a ship captain who was lost at sea before it was finished; a decade later it came into possession of the prominent Cushing family, which occupied it for 132 years. Longtime Historical Society member Margaret W. Cushing was born in the house, and when she passed away in 1955, at the age of 100, her heirs donated the house to the society. It was declared a National Historic Landmark in 1974.

Society collections include thousands of paintings, photographs, decorative arts and documents, but the house itself may be the most elegant artifact of all. Margaret Cushing saw no need to add modern conveniences to the house, and many decorative elements remained in place at her death, offering an unusual window into the past. Also on the property are large gardens that have been restored in part to what they might have looked like in the mid-1800s. A carriage house features a sleigh and other large artifacts from the society's collection.

Just steps away on Fruit Street is the Perkins Printing and Engraving Plant, known locally as "the Mint." Massachusetts currency was printed here for 23 years, beginning in 1809. The Historical Society acquired the property in 2008 and has since been engaged in restoration.

A short walk from downtown, the museum is generally open June through October. Call for hours, dates and special programs.

98 High St., Newburyport
978-462-2681
www.newburyhist.org

Custom House Maritime Museum

It's difficult to miss this imposing stone building just steps outside Market Square, especially with the two large, red-and-white buoys sitting out front.

Newburyport was a busy port in 1835, when the Custom House was built to provide a place where cargoes could be assessed and taxes collected. The building was designed by Robert Mills, architect of the Washington Monument and U.S. Treasury Building, and features the vaulted ceilings and cantilevered stone staircase that were among his trademarks. Many of the floors are brick. It's worth visiting for the architecture alone, but there's plenty of history here as well, in both permanent and changing exhibits.

The galleries boast a fleet of ship models, including one of the famously fast, built-in-Newburyport clipper the Dreadnought. A diorama of the nineteenth-century Currier Shipyard gives a glimpse of the local waterfront at its busiest. One room highlights Newburyport's role in the birth of the Coast Guard, which maintains a working station a short walk to the east (not open to the public). Another features shipwreck and salvage items from off the coast. Keep an eye on the paintings throughout, including Clement Drew's dramatic "Ship At Sea" and a harbor view attributed to Fitz Henry Lane.

The Marquand Library focuses on the family legacy of John P. Marquand, the Pulitzer prize-winning novelist who was a descendant of eighteenth-century shipping magnate Daniel Marquand and made Newburyport his home for much of the twentieth.

Newburyport's prominent role in the maritime trade had ended by the dawn of the twentieth century, and the Custom House passed into private hands. For decades the building was used for light manufacturing and storage, and even held the parts of a small submarine (!) that belonged to one owner. Damage and disrepair unfortunately resulted.

The Newburyport Maritime Society was founded in 1968 to protect, preserve and share the maritime heritage of the Merrimack Valley and its role in American history. Restoring the Custom House, which had its grand opening as a museum on June 28, 1975, was the centerpiece of that effort.

Full-price adult admission is $7. The museum is open seasonally, but year-round hours are said to be in the plans.

25 Water St., Newburyport
978-462-8681
www.customhousemaritimemuseum.org

Firehouse Center for the Arts

It really was a firehouse – you can tell by the tower once used for drying hoses. The original structure was built as a market and lyceum in 1823, and hosted such distinguished speakers as Ralph Waldo Emerson, Daniel Webster and Oliver Wendell Holmes. With additions, it served as the city's Central Fire Station from the mid-1800s until 1980.

After a grassroots community effort and major renovation, the building reopened as an arts center in 1991. The 195-seat theater on the upper floor offers plays, concerts, dance performances and other events throughout the year. The ground floor offers a gallery with rotating exhibits by North Shore artists and a restaurant with a popular open-air patio overlooking Market Square.

1 Market Square, Newburyport
978-462-7336
www.firehouse.org

Joppa Flats Education Center

Mass Audubon built the center on the edge of the Great Marsh in 2003, in part to serve the many visitors to Parker River National Wildlife Refuge on nearby Plum Island. It's just across the street from the refuge visitor center.

Birds are a focus here, as the adjacent marsh and estuary offer a stunning variety of resident and migratory populations. Bird-watchers can sight waterfowl, egrets, herons and even bald eagles over the Merrimack River without leaving the center. But Audubon staff load visitors into vans here for bird-watching trips to the refuge and other destinations. Bird counts, bird-a-thons and visits to Audubon's bird-banding station in the refuge are other popular activities.

Audubon staff host many education programs on the local ecosystem and its inhabitants. A marine touch tank, a butterfly garden, native plantings and other exhibits offer visitors a chance to learn before they go. There's a gift shop with everything from t-shirts to optics for birders. And the center is increasingly focused on its own role in the environment, with solar power and an electric car charging station.

1 Plum Island Turnpike, Newburyport
978-462-9998
www.massaudubon.org

Maudslay State Park

It's easy to get lost on the winding trails of Maudslay State Park, which covers nearly 500 hilly acres of the former Moseley family estate along the south bank of the Merrimack River. Created by the state in 1985, the park is divided between the remains of the formal landscaping to the west and woods and fields to the east. The park's most striking feature may be the river view from its bluffs. Bald eagles sometimes nest in the trees here.

Most of the estate's buildings, including the two main houses, are gone now. The entrance gate remains, as well as gardens, an on-site farm and various outbuildings. Trail walking and horseback riding are popular activities, and bicycles are permitted in the eastern part of the park. Rhododendrons bloom across vast swaths of the park's woods in the spring.

Since 1987 the Theater in the Open troupe has been headquartered in a former gatehouse at the eastern edge of Maudslay. In summer the group provides open-air performances for adults and children and youth theater camps. An annual highlight is their "Maudslay is Haunted" fund-raising weekend just before Halloween, in which visitors tour a series of macabre skits staged around the park.

A short bike ride or drive away is Moseley Woods, a 16-acre town park that was originally part of the same estate. Known as Moseley Pines to longtime residents, it offers wooded paths popular with hikers and dog-walkers, plus a playground, pavilion and picnic tables at a river overlook.

Maudslay State Park
Curzon Mill Road, Newburyport
978 465-7223
www.mass.gov/dcr

Moseley Woods
14 Spofford St., Newburyport
www.moseleywoods.com

APPENDICES
&
MISCELLANY

FIVE PLACES TO VISIT JUST OFF THE BYWAY

Lowell's Boat Shop
Amesbury

The oldest continuously operating boat shop in America.

Cross the Merrimack River from Newburyport on the historic Chain Bridge, then turn left into Amesbury's Point Shore neighborhood. Soon you'll encounter the rambling red building of Lowell's perched on the riverbank. Here skilled craftsmen and eager apprentices build dories and other small craft much as they have since 1793.

Family history credits founder Simeon Lowell with the "surf dory" design that was a major improvement on existing models, creating a rugged, eminently seaworthy craft that was also economical to build. The U.S. Life Saving Service used the surf dory in coastal rescue operations for almost a century.

Simeon's grandson Hiram Lowell designed the Banks Dory favored by Gloucester fishermen. Being a doryman was a grueling and highly hazardous way to make a living, but the sturdy Banks Dory became popular enough to make Lowell's the leading dory-builder in America in the late nineteenth century.

At its peak, in 1911, Lowell's produced 2,029 boats. But as the fishing industry changed, the dory business declined, sometimes precipitously, during the following decades.

As a non-profit working museum, Lowell's became a National Historic Landmark in 1990, under the auspices of the Newburyport Maritime Society. Since 2007, Lowell's has been run by the independent Lowell's Maritime Foundation.

Staff and volunteers welcome drop-in visitors. Boat-building classes and a variety of educational programs are offered throughout the year. Become a museum member and you'll even get to row a dory on the river.

Downtown Amesbury is certainly worth a visit too, with its restored millyards, lively restaurant scene and the John Greenleaf Whittier Home (*whittierhome.org*). Drive west from Lowell's, cross the Powow River, and follow Main Street north into town.

459 Main St., Amesbury
978-834-0050
www.lowellsboatshop.com

Nahant

Nahant residents like their quiet, little island-like community just the way it is, and there's not much here for the traveler. But it's worth a drive up Nahant Road to East Point just to look at the lovely old homes and occasional sea views.

Connected to Lynn by a narrow causeway, Nahant has roughly 3,500 residents in just 1.2 square miles. The land was first used for grazing cattle in the 1630s, and settlement was sparse until it became a resort community in the 1800s, home to several large hotels, now long gone. Nahant incorporated as a separate town in 1853.

One of the few public attractions on Nahant is Henry Cabot Lodge Park on East Point, with paths and benches on a rocky promontory. In the mid-1800s, this was the site of the three-hundred-room Nahant Hotel, which burned down in 1861. John E. Lodge bought the property and built homes there for his children, Senator Henry Cabot Lodge and Elizabeth Cabot Lodge. At the start of World War II, the military took over the property for artillery and fortifications intended to protect Boston Harbor from U-boats and other threats. In the 1950s, a Cold War Nike missile site was built there.

In 1967, Northeastern University acquired much of the property for what is now its Marine Science Center. The site offers panoramic water views, and World War II lookout towers still loom nearby. The park is accessed through the gates of the science center. Parking is limited without a resident sticker, as it also tends to be at beaches here.

Visitors to Nahant are welcome Wednesday and Thursday afternoons at the Nahant Historical Society in the Nahant Community

Center. The society offers exhibits on town history and a small book and gift shop.

41 Valley Road, Nahant
781-581-2727
www.nahanthistory.org

Peabody Historical Society
Peabody

When borders were first laid out in the 1620s, what is now called Peabody was part of Salem, so it seems appropriate to include its past here. The Peabody Historical Society and Museum maintains eight historic properties in town.

The society's main campus is on Washington Street, just outside Peabody Square, a few minutes' drive from downtown Salem. The 1810 General Gideon Foster House is the organization's headquarters and showcases items from the permanent collection, including china, textiles and fine and decorative arts, as well as local citizens' military artifacts from the Revolution to the Iraq war. The 1860 Osborne-Salata House next door houses the Elizabeth Cassidy Folk Art Museum, the Ruth Hill Library and Archives, and the Peabody Art Association gallery. Both historic homes play host to special exhibits such as the recent Art & Sole, which combined antique shoes from the collection, many locally made, with new works of art in a variety of media.

The Society also owns the George Peabody Birthplace and Library and Peabody Leatherworkers Museum at 205 Washington, which is open limited hours, and the Peabody Historical Fire Museum, open by appointment.

The Society's three other historic houses and the Smith Barn are over on the other side of Route 128, at the town-operated, 250-acre Brooksby Farm. The houses are open by appointment; the barn can be rented out for community and private events and hosts the Society's annual craft fair each October. Brooksby is a 250-acre working farm where you can pick your own apples, shop the farm stand, visit the petting zoo and hike or cross-country ski wooded trails.

Tours of the Society's properties and use of the library and archives are all free, though donations are "greatly appreciated." Some programs carry an admission charge for non-members.

35 Washington St., Peabody
978-531-0805
www.peabodyhistorical.org

Salisbury Beach State Reservation
Salisbury

Directly across the Merrimack River from the northern tip of Plum Island, this 521-acre park offers swimming, boating, fishing and camping. It has beaches on both the ocean and river, although dangerous currents and boat traffic bar swimming on the river side. Horseback riding is permitted in some areas.

Nearly 500 campsites make the reservation a busy place on summer weekends. Large parking lots, a picnic pavilion and new bathrooms accommodate day-trippers. Boat ramps on the marsh side of the park serve fishermen and recreational boaters.

One distinctly unusual feature on the river side of the reservation is known as "Butler's Toothpick." The tall, pyramidal structure was first built in 1873 as a navigational aid, and has been rebuilt at least once since. The Butler in question is Benjamin Franklin Butler, a military and political figure who was governor of Massachusetts in 1883-84. Why this object was named for him, though, remains unclear.

The reservation is still worth a visit during the off-season, when the campground is closed. Many of the same migrating bird species that make Plum Island National Wildlife Refuge a popular destination are often seen here. In the winter a colony of harbor seals and gray seals makes its home in the mouth of the river. Come on a bright day at low tide and you'll find them sunning themselves by the dozens on small rock islands just off the beach.

A short drive or a hike along the beach from the reservation is the center of Salisbury Beach, a classic American beach resort with arcades and snack bars. But the big amusement park rides are long

138

gone, and the center is no longer the gaudy magnet for families, and teens that it once was. A few new restaurants, a concert hall and condominiums suggest a slightly more upscale future.

To reach the reservation from the Byway, cross the river from Newburyport on Route 1 north over the Gillis Bridge to downtown Salisbury and turn right on Beach Road/Route 1A east. There is a per-car admission charge between Memorial Day and Labor Day, and other charges for camping.

Beach Road/Route 1A, Salisbury
978 462-4481
www.mass.gov/dcr

Saugus Iron Works
Saugus

The Saugus Iron Works National Historic Site is a worthy detour for any Byway visitor interested in the early days of the Massachusetts Bay Colony.

Less than 20 years after Boston was founded, Puritans here established what was then a sophisticated iron-making factory, which operated from 1646-1668 and helped set the young nation in motion by providing hammers, nails, pots and pans and other essentials.

The operation on site today is a reconstruction, based on mid-twentieth-century archaeological digs at the site and historic documents. It includes a working forge, rolling mill and large waterwheels used to power the manufacture of cast and wrought iron products.

Also present is the "Iron Works House" a timber-framed, 1680s mansion on its original location. It was constructed about a decade after the iron works ceased production. The site by the Saugus River is also a rich habitat for wildlife. Open seasonally.

244 Central St., Saugus
781-233-0050
www.nps.gov

ITINERARIES, & LISTS

The Art Lover's Weekend
on Cape Ann

Having booked two nights in a Gloucester inn, arrive on Saturday morning and start with a stroll around Fitz Henry Lane's solemn stone house on the waterfront (page 68). Don't miss the statue of the artist there.

Then walk straight up the hill on Pleasant Street to the Cape Ann Museum (page 64) and search out Lane's work in the galleries, including his early panorama of Gloucester Harbor and his atmospheric painting of Brace's Rock on Eastern Point.

After lunch, drive to East Gloucester and walk the Rocky Neck Historic Art Trail to see sites relating to Edward Hopper, Marsden Hartley and more (page 75). Visit the Rocky Neck Art Colony gallery. If you're lucky, you'll find artists holding open studios.

Dine in one of the restaurants on Rocky Neck Avenue overlooking Smith Cove. Then, if you come in season, take in a play at Gloucester Stage (page 70) just across the water.

On Sunday after breakfast, head north to Dogtown (page 66) to hunt down Babson's Boulders and savor the atmosphere that so inspired Hartley. Then drive on to Rockport for lunch and spend an afternoon browsing the Rockport Art Association (page 84) and other local galleries.

After dinner at one of many local restaurants, take in a concert at the Shalin Liu Performance Center (page 85) before heading back to your lodgings.

You'll want to book the play and concert ahead; if you have to book a concert on Saturday, just switch days. Gloucester Stage usually has late-afternoon matinees on Sundays.

The Nature Lover's Weekend
On the North Shore

First of all, don't do this during the midsummer greenhead fly season. Early or late in the summer are better choices, when migrations are at their peak.

Start with an early morning bird-watching tour with the staff from Mass Audubon's Joppa Flats Education Center (page 130) in Newburyport. They may take you to Plum Island or another nearby location, but they know where to find the best looks, and if there's a rarity passing through, they'll know about it.

When you get back, cross the road to the Parker River National Wildlife Refuge headquarters (page 118) to learn about the ecology and wildlife of the Great Marsh (page 116).

In the afternoon or evening, depending on the tides, it's time to see the marsh close up. Head out with Plum Island Kayak (page 149), which actually launches from downtown Newburyport, to paddle the Plum Island estuary. Or paddle off with ERBA (page 149), which launches in downtown Essex, and explore the Essex River estuary. Either way, you'll see diverse ecosystems in buzzing life. You might see an otter swim past, or a striped bass break the surface. Herons, egrets, osprey and even eagles may make appearances. And you'll be right in the middle of their world, not watching it on TV.

Pro tip: Schedule your kayak paddle first, because their timing and route is determined by the tides.

After a few hours of paddling in the sun, you'll probably be ready to call it a day and search out a cold beverage. That's fine, but get to bed early, because you don't want to be tired for day two.

You'll want to be at full-strength for your whale watching adventure, whether you sail from Newburyport, Gloucester or Salem (On The Water, page 148). Get to the dock early, and bring a fleece or a jacket, even if it's warm where you are, because conditions out on the ocean are often very different from those on land. Most boats have snack bars and even a limited selection of adult beverages onboard. Check your boat's policy before bringing your own food or drink.

Don't forget your camera – but unless photography is really your thing, don't spend all your time looking through the lens.

You'll motor for an hour or two after leaving the dock. I always stay outside on the deck, enjoying the ocean views and wildlife ranging from seabirds diving for fish to dolphins jumping alongside the boat. But if you stay on the deck all that time, you can also be cold, wind-burned and damp with salt spray by the time you get near your quarry.

Several types of whales feed off the New England Coast, primarily humpbacks, finbacks and minkes. Whale-watch captains will try to get you as close as they can without violating the federally protected creatures' personal space. Sometimes you'll take a cruise where all you see is a minke or two shooting across the surface like a torpedo a few hundred yards away. On another trip you'll be dazzled by the curious and even playful behavior of a pod of humpbacks that seems intent on giving you your money's worth. For many people a successful whale watch is the highlight of their year.

Pro tip: By the time the boat is near whales, you should have stationed yourself in the pulpit on the bow of the boat, or, second choice, at the stern. That way you have the widest range of vision, so you can see the whales wherever they surface around you.

Eventually the whales will move on, and your captain will set a course for home. There is no shame in resting inside the cabin or even napping a little on the way in. The salt air will do that to you.

A day for wooden boat lovers

Here's one trip that should go north to south.

Start just off the Byway at Lowell's Boat Shop in Amesbury (page 135), with a look at their traditional dory-building operation. You might even get hands-on. Every time I'm there, they ask me to help move a boat on the sawhorses.

Then drive on down to Essex and visit the Essex Shipbuilding Museum (page 92). Make sure you take a look across the inlet at Harold Burnham's boatyard, too. By now it's time for lunch, but keep an eye on your watch, because you'll have already booked an afternoon sail on the Burnham-built schooner Ardelle (page 148) out of Maritime Gloucester (page 72).

I've got a soft spot for the Ardelle, having seen its launch, but there are many other options in our On The Water section (page 148).

If there's any time left, or tomorrow, check out the Custom House Maritime Museum in Newburyport (page 128), the Cape Ann Museum in Gloucester (page 64) or the Peabody Essex Museum in Salem. (page 41) All have maritime collections that will interest you as well.

Home sweet homes

There are numerous historic homes on the Byway, but a handful are known far and wide for their architecture or their décor, the artifacts or history collected in their rooms. The five must-see houses on the Byway are:

1) The House of Seven Gables, Salem (page 39)
2) Beauport, Gloucester (page 62)
3) Cogswell's Grant, Essex (page 90)
4) Castle Hill, Crane Estate, Ipswich (page 99)
5) Spencer-Peirce-Little Farm, Newbury (page 111)

Life's a beach

You've had enough history and nature, and now you want to kick back on the sand and snooze behind your Kindle. Pack the sunscreen and head for one of these five top beaches on the Byway:

1) Nahant Beach Reservation, Lynn/Nahant (page 18)
2) Singing Beach, Manchester-by-the-Sea (page 58)
3) Good Harbor Beach, Gloucester (page 70)
4) Crane Beach, Crane Estate, Ipswich (page 100)
5) Parker River National Wildlife Refuge (page 118)

Where to take the kids

The North Shore is not awash in kid-friendly amusement parks with roller coasters and water slides. That's just not our style. You can try Salem Willows amusement park (*www.salemwillowspark.com*) or Salisbury Beach for arcade games and the like. But the following attractions will entertain school-age kids and maybe even teach them something:

1) Salem Witch Museum (page 46, for kids 6+)
2) Maritime Gloucester (page 72)
3) The Parker River National Wildlife Refuge headquarters, Newburyport (page 118)
4) A whale watch (page 148)
5) For teenagers, a kayak trip (page 148)

You can spend a whole day...

...exploring the collections of the Peabody Essex Museum.

...absorbing everything witch-related in Salem, solemn to silly.

...at the Crane Estate in Ipswich, touring Castle Hill, hiking the trails and lolling on the beach.

...without talking to another person, if you walk far enough down the beach at the Parker River National Wildlife Refuge on Plum Island.

...trying to find your way back to your car at Dogtown in Gloucester. (Just kidding.) (Not really.)

BYWAY VISITOR CENTERS

Lynn Museum & Historical Society (Year-round)
590 Washington St., Lynn. 781-581-6200, www.lynnmuseum.com

Marblehead Information Booth (May to October)
Pleasant and Spring Streets, Marblehead. 781-631-2868,
www.visitmarblehead.com

National Park Service Regional Visitor Center (Year-round)
2 New Liberty St., Salem. 978-740-1650, www.nps.gov

Gloucester Visitor Welcoming Center (May to October)
Stage Fort Park, Hough Avenue, Gloucester. 978-281-8865,
www.essexheritage.org

Rockport Information Center (May to October)
Upper Main Street (Rt. 127), Rockport. 978-283-1601,
www.rockportusa.com

Custom House Maritime Museum (April to December)
25 Water St., Newburyport. 978-462-8681,
www.customhousemaritimemuseum.org

Ipswich Visitor Center (May-October)
Hall Haskell House, 36 S. Main Street, Ipswich. 978-356-8540,
www.ipswichma.com

Maria Miles Visitor Information Center (Year-round)
I-95 Southbound, Exit 60, Salisbury. 978-465-6555,
www.northofbostoncvb.org

THE BYWAY BY TRAIN OR BICYCLE

Ten of the thirteen Byway communities can be reached by MBTA commuter rail. The Newburyport/Rockport Line leaves from Boston's North Station and stops in Lynn, Swampscott, Salem and Beverly before splitting in two. From there, some trains go on to Ipswich, Rowley and Newburyport, others to Manchester-by-the-Sea, Gloucester and Rockport. The sales agent can help you choose the right train when you buy your ticket at North Station. Round trips currently cost from $12 (Lynn) to $20 (Newburyport or Rockport). Details and schedules are at *www.mbta.com.*

The Salem, Gloucester and Ipswich train stations are close enough to downtown destinations to be an easy stroll. In Manchester-by-the-Sea, it's a half-mile walk to Singing Beach. Downtown Newburyport is about a mile from the station, but there's a pleasant, paved walking trail dotted with public sculptures.

Even in those communities, however, many popular attractions – Beauport and Castle Hill, for example – are miles from the stations and not really walkable. Taxi or bus service may fill the gap, but advance planning is required.

Marblehead, Essex and Newbury are not on the commuter rail at all, nor is Plum Island.

If you want to enjoy the Byway without a car, of course, there's another option: Ride a bicycle. Just about any part of the Byway is bike-able, especially for an experienced rider. As with many old New England communities, though, the roads tend to be curvy and crowded.

Popular rides include: Route 127 through Manchester and the Magnolia section of Gloucester (take a detour down the side roads near Hammond Castle); the Back Shore of Gloucester and Rockport; and Route 127 north from Rockport into the Gloucester villages of Lanesville and Annisquam. The Parker River National Wildlife Refuge on Plum Island offers several miles of relatively flat travel.

There are also major mountain biking destinations in the area, notably Lynn Woods and Gloucester's Dogtown.

You can drive to your starting point, of course, but it's worth noting that the commuter rail has been increasingly bicycle-friendly, offering special bike coaches on the Newburyport/Rockport Line on weekends and holidays. Consult *www.mbta.com* for details.

There are several groups that offer helpful information and organized rides, including the North Shore Cyclists (*www.nscyc.org*), Mass Bike (*massbike.org*), the Greater Boston chapter of the New England Mountain Bike Association (*www.gbnemba.org*), and, for racers, Essex County Velo (*ecvcycling.org*).

ON THE WATER

One of the best ways to enjoy the North Shore is to get out on the water, whether sailing the Atlantic or paddling the Great Marsh. What follows is a subjective selection of sail and cruise opportunities, whale watches and kayak outfitters.

Most go out only seasonally. Many offer special sunset, holiday or music cruises as well as charters. Novices are welcome on most guided kayak tours. But for all of these activities, you should definitely call ahead or book online. (See page 141 for tips on enjoying your whale watch.)

I haven't tried to list party-fishing boats and fishing charters, because there are simply too many from which to choose. Ask for a recommendation at the local bait and tackle shop.

Adventure/Gloucester

This 122-foot, 1926 fishing schooner once took Gloucestermen to sea to fish from small dories. Public sails are set to begin in spring 2013. *978-281-8079, www.schooner-adventure.org*

Ardelle/Gloucester

The 57-foot, 49-passenger pinky schooner launched in Essex in 2011 and sails daily from Maritime Gloucester. *978-290-7168, schoonerardelle.com*

Cape Ann Harbor Tours/Gloucester

Cape Ann and lobstering tours and a harbor shuttle. *978-283-1979, www.capeannharbortours.com*

Capt. Bill and Sons/Gloucester

Daily whale-watch trips on the 100-foot Miss Cape Ann. In business for 50 years. *800-339-4253, www.captbillandsons.com*

Discovery Adventures/Gloucester
Kayak Ipswich Bay and the ocean from Lane's Cove on Cape Ann.
978-283-3320, discoadventures.com

ERBA/Essex
Essex River Basin Adventures offers lessons and guided tours in the Great Marsh and beyond.
978-768-3722, www.erba.com

Essex River Cruises & Charters/Essex
Narrated marsh tours, beach clambakes, charters and more.
800-748-3706, www.essexcruises.com

Fame/Salem
Sail on a replica of an early-1800s Chebacco fishing schooner that turned privateer in the war of 1812. Launched in Essex in 2003.
800-979-3370, www.schoonerfame.com

Ninth Wave/Newburyport
A personal favorite. Sailing on this 48-foot, 48-passenger catamaran is a unique experience. Get comfortable in the nets once they turn off the engines (but empty your pockets first).
866-984-9283, www.9thwave.net

North Shore Kayak Outdoor Center/Rockport
Sea kayak tours leaving daily from Bearskin Neck.
978-546-5050, www.northshorekayak.com

Plum Island Kayak/Newburyport
Rentals and guided tours. The sunset seal paddles are our favorite.
978-462-5510, www.plumislandkayak.com

Prince of Whales/Newburyport
Whale-watching trips with experts from the Blue Ocean Society.
800-848-1111, www.newburyportwhalewatch.com

Salem Kayak
Guided tours both scheduled and on demand.
978-270-8170, www.kayaksalem.com

7 Seas Whale Watch/Gloucester
Onboard the 108-foot Privateer IV. A recent Yankee Magazine editor's choice.
888-283-1776, www.7seas-whalewatch.com

Thomas E. Lannon/Gloucester
Daily sails from Seven Seas Wharf on a 65-foot schooner launched in Essex in 1997.
978-281-6634, www.schooner.org

Yankee Clipper/Newburyport
Merrimack River and Great Marsh eco-tours.
603-682-2293, www.harbortours.com

SELECTED
BIBLIOGRAPHY

- Bierfelt, Kristin. *The North Shore Literary Trail* (History Press, 2009)
- Craig, James A. *Fitz H. Lane: An Artist's Voyage Through Nineteenth-Century America* (History Press, 2006)
- Daily News of Newburyport. *Port in Progress* (Pediment Publishing, 2008)
- Diamant, Anita. *The Last Days of Dogtown* (Scribner, 2005)
- East, Elyssa. *Dogtown: Death and Enchantment in a New England Ghost Town* (Free Press, 2009)
- Garland, Joseph E. *Eastern Point: A Nautical, Rustical and More or Less Sociable Chronicle of Gloucester's Outer Shield and Inner Sanctum, 1606–1990*, Joseph Garland (Commonwealth Editions, 1999)
- Garland, Joseph E. *The Gloucester Guide: A Stroll Through Place and Time* (History Press, 2004)
- Garland, Joseph E. *The North Shore: A Social History of Summers Among the Noteworthy, Fashionable, Rich, Eccentric and Ordinary on Boston's Gold Coast, 1820–1929* (Commonwealth Editions, 1998)
- Gellerman, Bruce, and Sherman, Erik. *Massachusetts Curiosities: Quirky Characters, Roadside Oddities & Other Offbeat Stuff* (Globe Pequot Press, 2005)
- Groff, Bethany. *A Brief History of Old Newbury* (History Press, 2008)
- Harrison, Nancy Jo T., and Woodward, Jean L., editors. *Along the Coast of Essex County* (Junior League of Boston, 1971)
- Holt, Stephen Roberts. *Manchester-By-The-Sea* (Images of America series, Arcadia Publishing, 2009)
- Junger, Sebastian. *The Perfect Storm: A True Story of Men Against the Sea* (W. W. Norton & Company, 1997)

- Lindborg, Kristina. *A Natural History of Boston's North Shore* (University Press of New England, 2007)
- Mann, Charles E. *In The Heart Of Cape Ann, Or, The Story Of Dogtown* (Procter Brothers, 1896, via Google Books)
- National Park Service. *Salem: Maritime Salem in the Age of Sail,* aka *Handbook 126* (National Park Service, Division of Publications, 1987)
- Pringle, James R. *History of the town and city of Gloucester, Cape Ann, Massachusetts*, (The City of Gloucester Archives Committee, 1997)
- Sherman, Paul. *Big Screen Boston* (Black Bars Publishing, 2008)
- Vincent, L.M.. *In Search of Motif No. 1: The History of a Fish Shack* (History Press, 2011)
- Wilhelm, Robert. *Murder and Mayhem in Essex County* (History Press, 2011)
- Wilmerding, John. *Fitz Hugh Lane* (Praeger Publishers, 1971)

ACKNOWLEDGMENTS

Many, many people helped make this book happen by offering encouragement, advice, information and time out of their busy days. Any errors or omissions are mine alone.

Annie Harris, Bill Steelman, Deb Payson and Emily Levin at the Essex National Heritage Commission were the first to offer their support, which has come in too many ways to list here.

Answers, feedback and access were provided by Courtney Richardson and Martha Oaks at the Cape Ann Museum; Michael Mroz at the Custom House Maritime Museum in Newburyport; Ed Becker and Mary Williamson at Essex County Greenbelt Association; Justin Demetri at the Essex Shipbuilding Museum; Bethany Groff and Julie Arrison of Historic New England; Tom Balf at Maritime Gloucester; Bill Gette and Michael O'Connor at Mass Audubon; April Swieconek, Whitney Van Dyke and David Thibodeau at the Peabody Essex Museum; David Beardsley, Kristi Perri, Brian Degasperis and Russell Hopping at the Trustees of Reservations.

Also: Joey Ciaramitaro at Good Morning Gloucester, Abby Battis at the Lynn Museum; authors Anita Diamant, Elyssa East, and Lawrence Vincent; John G. Stoffolano, Jr., Professor of Entomology at UMass Amherst; Laurie Fullerton at Burnham shipyard; Kristen Cunha at the House of Seven Gables; Jean Adams at Parker River National Wildlife Refuge; Wendy Evans at the Ipswich Museum; Pam Peterson at the Marblehead Museum; and Karen Herlitz of Rockport Music. No doubt there are more whom I have accidentally omitted, for which I beg their pardon.

Thanks to all of our local booksellers for their support.

Kerry Drohan and Marcia Dick of the *Boston Globe* assigned me to stories all over the North Shore and said yes to many of my pitches. Without them, this book would never have been written.

Cover designer Greg Freeman, artist Dylan Metrano and copy editor Bill Brotherton have been creative and patient throughout the project, as well as exceedingly generous with their time.

As always, I am grateful to my parents for pens and paper, books and magazines.

Last but most important is Rosemary Krol, my sounding board, first editor and essential support in every way.

Supporters

Without these people, who were most generous in supporting my Kickstarter.com campaign in summer 2012, this book might not exist. So I am very sincerely grateful to:

Rick and Elizabeth Patenaude
Nancy Brown and Judy Coburn
Sandra Brown
Heather Shand

Chip Hersey and M.J. Benson, Judy and David Chesney, Mark and Corrie, Brian and Dawne and Mae, George McQuilken, Joyce Richmond, Ruth and Peter Riley, Michael Sprague, Bill Steelman and Sue Hertz.

Elliot and Christa Brown, Heather Cathcart of WhatsTheSoup, Mike and Rich, Michael Gagne, Sue Grenier, Erica Holthausen, Philip Jacob and Béatrice Peltre, my friend at JogNog.com, Alan D. Nasberg, Bill and Jennifer Perry with Kasey and Jamal Holland and Rebecca Perry and Justin Sessions, Helen Pinsky, Walter and Helen Renaud, the Rooney family, Eric Savage, Halley Suitt Tucker.

And to all the other folks who backed this project, thank you, and your books are on the way!

About the artist

Dylan Metrano grew up in Newburyport, and has been paper-cutting for more than ten years. He is self-taught, a member of the Newburyport Art Association and the Rockport Art Association, and a co-founder of the Free Art Show. Dylan's art is cut from paper with an X-Acto knife, and carefully layered. He has designed numerous album covers, book covers, posters and an occasional pet portrait.

metrano.wix.com/papercutting
www.facebook.com/papercutting

Photo credits

Page 15, photography by Jeff Dykes, courtesy of the Lynn Museum & Historical Society. Page 89, by Len Burgess, courtesy of the photographer. Page 114 and 123, by the author.

Courtesy of Essex National Heritage Commission: Page 22, photo by Jayson Mitchell. Pages 27 and 97, Greg Mazzotta. Page 35, Rod Parker. Page 49, Marissa Mariano. Page 55, Julie Freitas. Page 60, Dick Scott. Page 79, Alan Joslin. Page 105, Elizabeth Marshall. Page 108, Marion Bayly.

Author photo, page 156, by Rosemary Krol.

About the author

Joel Brown has been a correspondent for the *Boston Globe* since 2005, while writing for many other publications and websites. Previously, he was a reporter and/or editor for the *Boston Herald, Electronic Media*, the *Daily Southtown* and the *Recorder*. He has also published two mysteries about a place called "Libertyport," *Mirror Ball Man* and *Mermaid Blues,* with a third due in 2013. He is a Massachusetts native, a lifelong Red Sox fan, and a resident of Newburyport since 1998.

jbnbpt@gmail.com
www.facebook.com/JoelBrownauthor

14951565R00083

Made in the USA
Charleston, SC
09 October 2012